# British *Muslims* *and* *Schools*

British Library Cataloguing-in-Publication Data
A catalogue record of this book is available from the British Library


3rd Revised and expanded Edition 2004
ISBN 0 907261 43 4


*Published by:*
**The Muslim Educational Trust**
130 Stroud Green Road
London N4 3RZ
UK
Tel: 020 7272 8502
Fax: 020 7281 3457
www.muslim-ed-trust.org.uk
email: info@muslim-ed-trust.org.uk


**ISBN 0 907261 43 4**

*Printed and bound in Great Britain by:*
Hobbs The Printer
Brunel Road
Totton, Hampshire
SO40 3WX
Tel: 023 8066 4800 Fax: 023 8066 4801
http://www.hobbs.co.uk

# Contents

In the name of Allāh, The Most Merciful, The Most Kind

## PREFACE TO THE REVISED AND EXPANDED EDITION

All praise is for Allāh, the revised second edition of my book *British Muslims and Schools* has sold out. I thought it is essential to revise the book to reflect the numerous changes in legislation since the last edition. The book seeks to promote a better understanding of the educational needs of British Muslims and suggest ways and means to tackle them with sensitivity, empathy, and positive action, thus improving the overall quality of education.

I hope this revised and expanded edition will continue to assist education policy-makers, including the Department for Education and Skills (DfES), the Qualifications and Curriculum Authority (QCA), Local Education Authorities (LEAs) and schools, to understand the issues discussed and adopt measures to help develop an equitable system of education ensuring equal opportunities for all and improving standards in all areas of education. In addition, it should also help British Muslim parents, organisations and children to be aware of their rights and responsibilities.

In Islām, education is viewed as a process through which a child is prepared for this life and the afterlife so that the child can face life situations with an awareness of responsibility and accountability. Islām requires all human endeavours to conform to Qur'ānic Guidance which is immutable, infallible and valid for all times and climes. The use, method and manner of a particular area of study determine its acceptability; this is the principle used when considering such areas of a broad and balanced curriculum as physical education, swimming, art, music, dance and Sex and Relationship education (SRE).

I have benefitted from the comments and suggestions of Usamah K. Ward, Tahir Alam, Dr. M.K. Hasan, Dr. M. Akhtaruzzaman, M. Akram Khan-Cheema, Muhammed Ibrahim, and Ibrahim Hewitt. I am grateful to all of them.

I am also grateful to Muḥammad Al-Amin who has designed the text layout and the cover of this revised and expanded edition.

Finally, I implore Almighty Allāh, my Merciful Creator, to accept my humble efforts. Āmīn.

**Ghulam Sarwar**

24 Ramaðān 1425 AH

7 November 2004 CE

*In the name of Allåh, The Most Merciful, The Most Kind*

# British Muslims
# and Schools

## INTRODUCTION

There are nearly 2 million Muslims living in Britain, around half a million of whom are children of compulsory school age (5-16) attending maintained schools. Although Muslims live all over the country, they are largely concentrated in places such as London, Bradford, Birmingham, Manchester, Liverpool, Luton, Cardiff, Glasgow, Dewsbury, Rochdale, Oldham, Leicester, Sheffield, Huddersfield, Leeds, Preston, Nottingham, Wolverhampton, Walsall and so on.

Muslims are a distinct religious community with a way of life based on the Qur'ān (the final revealed Book of Allāh – God) and the Sunnah (example) of the final Prophet of Allāh, Muḥammad ﷺ. Although sharing common beliefs, Muslims originally came to Britain from many parts of the world; thus the community speaks many different languages and has diverse cultures and traditions.

It is widely recognised that Muslim children in Britain – most of whom have been born in this country – have distinct educational needs directly related to their faith and cultural heritage. Such needs should be acknowledged by local education authorities (LEAs) and catered for by schools if Muslim children are to achieve their full potential in British society. It is worth mentioning that some LEAs, including Manchester, Brent, Bradford, Birmingham, East Sussex and the now defunct Inner London Education Authority, have in the past issued guidelines on how schools should cater for the needs of their Muslim pupils. Despite such worthwhile initiatives and imaginative developments, much still remains to be done.

Since its formation in 1966, **The Muslim Educational Trust (MET)** has taken pioneering steps to suggest ways in which the needs of Muslim pupils can be met. The Trust's publications have been remarkably successful in developing empathy in the wider community and have generally raised the level of awareness amongst those responsible for providing education in our multifaith and multi-cultural society.

In this book, an attempt is made to highlight some of the educational concerns of the Muslim community, and the problems encountered in trying to overcome them in order to improve the quality of education for all. More importantly, suggestions are made which, if implemented, will allow an important section of British society to contribute fully to the society in which they live in an atmosphere of understanding and participation. Rather than looking at educational requests from Muslims with an unhelpful or hostile attitude, it would diffuse tension and remove misunderstanding if they are addressed with empathy, sincerity, mutual respect, and positive outlook.

Islām views education as a process through which a child's total personality is developed in preparation for this life *and* the Ākhirah (the life after death). Without belief in the pivotal concept of the Ākhirah, development of the feelings of responsibility *and ultimate accountability –* prerequisites of a stable, peaceful society – is not possible.

To a practising Muslim, life is a compact whole and inspiration is drawn from Allāh the Creator of us all, Who has neither partners nor equals. His Guidance is the criterion for the affairs of human life. Hence, the concerns mentioned in this booklet are not based on human thoughts or desires (which are fallible and prone to alteration) but on the Guidance of Allāh – infallible and everlasting.

Muslims find it difficult to accept some parts of the school curriculum, not because the subjects are prohibited *per se*, but because their methodology of teaching is against the Guidance of Allāh. The latter is the ultimate yardstick for Muslims.

Looked at from this angle, with understanding and sensitivity, it should be clear that Muslims do not ask for impossible concessions. On the contrary, it has to be agreed that most of the areas of concern and their remedies are academically, legally and socially sound. *After all, Muslim children are part and parcel of British society and the balanced growth of society as a whole is only possible when all sections of society have equal opportunities to employ their skills and potential for its overall well-being.*

## PARENTAL RIGHTS AND RESPONSIBILITIES

Numerous changes in legislation have improved the rights of parents concerning the choice of schools available to their children, information about schools, annual reports of the schools, pupils' progress reports, active participation in the running of schools as governors, the league tables published by DfES, etc. Some extracts from relevant education acts are reproduced in *Appendix I*.

Maintained, voluntary (Aided) and foundation schools are all legally obliged to provide parents with information about the school so that they can express informed preferences for the future education of their children. The law requires all relevant information about schools to be presented in such a way that the parents can understand it clearly, even if this means translating the booklets into the appropriate languages of the local community. As probably most Muslim parents are now born and educated in Britain, the need to provide interpreters during parent/teacher consultations would be at a much lesser scale than would be the case a decade earlier.

It is essential for Muslim parents to read brochures and other detailed information about schools carefully and consult with the head teacher of their chosen school about their children's particular requirements. If they are unable to communicate their concerns, Muslims should seek the help of an appropriately qualified fellow Muslim or a Muslim organisation which advises on such matters.

It is equally important for Muslims to take all possible measures to ensure that their children do not underachieve in schools. **Muslim parents should have high expectations of their children and encourage them to aim for excellence.** At the same time, we believe that the problems of inner-city life – unemployment, poor housing, general deprivation – should be addressed by the provision of additional resources. A report by the **Office for Standards in Education (Ofsted)** in October 1993 concluded that **schools need a systematic programme of improvement ... to retain the services of skilled teachers ... and to have higher expectations of children.** (*The Times Educational Supplement*, 29 October 1993) Thus, Government initiatives aimed at education in particular will help to redress the current imbalance in terms of access to opportunity for children from disadvantaged areas and families. Underachievement has to be tackled by the combined efforts of the authorities, schools *and* parents.

## COLLECTIVE WORSHIP (CW) AND SCHOOL ASSEMBLIES

Many parents, including Muslims, are unaware of the content of acts of Collective Worship and school assemblies. As a result, the decision to allow their children to attend such sessions is made without a clear awareness and understanding of what the school offers.

The Education Reform Act 1988 ammended by the Education Act 1996 Sec. 386 (c) makes it clear that schools must provide every pupil in attendance with a daily act of Collective Worship; the majority of such acts in any term should be **wholly or mainly of a broadly Christian character**. Relatively few schools have organiseded their Collective Worship in line with the requirements of the ERA and many find it difficult to implement the law. Those schools which organise their assemblies as per the requirement of the 1996 Act, find that these make positive contribution to the ethos of the school.

The general decline in religious practice, growth of secularism and presence of a variety of faith groups in many schools all complicate the issue of Collective Worship. **Schools find it more and more difficult to make worship appropriate and relevant for all children.**

**The Education Act 1944** gave parents the right to withdraw their children from religious assemblies (Section 25) and that right remained unchanged by the ERA and the Education Acts of 1993 and 1996. Indeed, the **Circular 1/94 on Religious Education and Collective Worship issued by the Department for Education and Employment (DFEE) in January 31, 1994** says that the right of withdrawal **should be freely exercisable and when exercised, the schools must give effect to any such request (para 85).** If parents so wish, they must give a withdrawal request in writing to the head teacher. The school must comply with that request and continues to be responsible for the supervision of any child so withdrawn from RE or Collective Worship [paras. 83 (2) and 84].

Although schools must respect and act upon requests for withdrawal from Collective Worship, some head teachers apply direct or indirect pressure on Muslim parents to make them change their minds. Since many Muslims are unaware of their legal rights, they may be swayed. Such an attitude is clearly unhelpful; head teachers should appreciate the religious concerns of parents when dealing with requests for withdrawal, and advise and assist them in taking advantage of their right. In schools where children are not made to attend Collective Worship based on a faith other than their own, a more positive atmosphere of empathy and understanding can be developed.

Some schools try to overcome such situations by organising non-religious or multicultural assemblies; post-ERA, of course, these do not meet the legal requirements except in certain circumstances (see the section on determinations below).

Muslim parents who are worried about the Collective Worship on offer in their children's school could opt for one of the following:

1. They can withdraw their children from Collective Worship. The children will then be supervised by the school and may rejoin the main assembly to hear school notices, etc.
2. If Muslim pupils are in a minority, they can be withdrawn from Collective Worship and the school can be requested to allow alternative Islāmic worship/assemblies on the school premises. These acts of worship would not be classed as statutory worship (the children having been withdrawn from that) and so are not bound by the law governing such worship. If any costs are incurred in arranging such alternative worship they must be borne by the parents and/or the local Muslim community.
3. If Muslims are in the majority in a school, it is clear that worship which is mainly Christian in character would be inappropriate. In such a situation, the head teacher – following consultation with the governing body and possibly the parents – **can apply to the local Standing Advisory Council on Religious Education (SACRE) for a determination that Christian worship is inappropriate for some or all of the pupils in the school.** If granted, the head teacher must arrange alternative *statutory* worship (as opposed to alternative

worship for those who have been withdrawn from the statutory worship) and this may be, for example, Islāmic worship. Non-Muslims would have the right to withdraw from such worship. If the determination has been obtained for part of the school, or a number of determinations have been granted for different groups within the school, acts of worship for each group can be arranged *(para. 79, Circular 1/94 on RE and CW).*

**It is our view that the procedure for seeking a determination is cumbersome. If the professional judgement of a head teacher is that Christian worship is inappropriate for some or all of the pupils in the school then that should be sufficient. The head teacher in consultation with the Board of Governors should be empowered to organise alternative worship if that is more suitable. If the majority of pupils in the school are Muslims the alternative should be Islāmic worship.**

### DETERMINATIONS

A determination is a legal decision made by the Standing Advisory Council on Religious Education (SACRE) to lift the requirement of **wholly or mainly of a broadly Christian Character** of Collective Worship for a school where a group of pupils or the majority of pupils are of non-Christian faith. Every LEA is legally required to constitute a SACRE. Determinations are usually granted for five years and head teachers can ask for review before that time, should circumstances require this. Determinations could be for the whole school or for a part of the school.

For schools with pupils from different faiths, e.g. Muslims, Hindus, Sikhs and Jews, a part school determination should be made as per the requirments of the appropriate Education Acts. **The broadly Christian Character** aspect will continue to operate for those pupils for whom it is appropriate.

**In the case of alternative statutory worship, any costs involved must be borne by the school, as the school is discharging its legal duty to provide worship for the pupils involved. This was confirmed by the then Minister of State for Education, Dame Angela Rumbold, in a letter to the Director of The Muslim Educational Trust in November**

**1989.** (*Appendix II*)

Despite there being clear provision in law and guidance from the DfES concerning alternatives to Christian worship, many schools with a majority of Muslim pupils simply carry on with assemblies which are in conflict with the law, making the well-intentioned but complicated provisions of the ERA meaningless. Whilst it is agreed that there are difficulties in putting legal theory into practice for Collective Worship, it should also be recognised that there is a general unwillingness to do so.

Muslim parents must realise that silence and inaction on their part can have serious long-term consequences for their children; they should make every effort to arrange for Islāmic Collective Worship in local schools which have a majority of Muslim pupils.

It should be the responsibility of every head teacher and governing body to review Collective Worship provision taking into consideration the age, cultural background and religious composition of the school population.

It is worth a mention here that some RE teachers and advisers may not like to see Islāmic acts of worship take place in schools. We would like them to appreciate that **pupils are to be educated according to the wishes of their parents (Section 9, 1996 Education Act) and urge them to respect the wishes of Muslim parents.**

## RELIGIOUS EDUCATION

Religious Education (RE) is taught in maintained schools according to a syllabus agreed locally. Voluntary and Foundation Schools may use the agreed syllabus of any LEA; but they are required to use a syllabus based on the terms of their trust deed. Since the ERA and later legislation, new syllabuses must **reflect the fact that the religious traditions in Great Britain are in the main Christian whilst taking account of the teaching and practices of the other principal religions represented in Great Britain.**

When deliberating upon the content of a syllabus for RE, a local Agreed Syllabus Conference must keep the legal requirements in mind as well as the wishes of the local community. This is especially important following the guidance given in the Circular 1/94 on RE and CW which stresses that the relative content devoted to Christianity in syllabuses must predominate (para. 34). Obviously, this causes problems in areas where non-Christians form the majority of school pupils.

**The Schools Curriculum and Assessment Authority (SCAA)** which has been replaced now by the **Qualifications and Curriculum Authority (QCA)** produced model RE syllabuses which may be used as a basis for locally agreed syllabuses *(Model syllabuses for Religious Education, Model 1 and 2, SCAA, 1994 reprinted by QCA, 1998).* We hope that these syllabuses do not become mandatory, undermining local needs. Included in the guidelines for the SCAA in drafting these models is that they must **reflect the fact … in the main Christian …** etc. while at the same time taking into account the national and local position of religions. Clearly, in areas with a high percentage of non-Christian pupils, matching these requirements may not be possible. Reaching agreement between all members of an Agreed Syllabus Conference may also be difficult.

The QCA has produced non-statutory guidelines for the teaching of RE, launched by **Charles Clarke**, the Secretary of State for Education and Skills on 28 October 2004. These guidelines might be made mandatory in the near future.

It may be worth mentioning at this point that Muslims have no difficulties studying other religious beliefs and practices; a serious study of the Qur'ān will, for example, lead naturally to a study of the 'People of the Book' (Jews and Christians). What causes difficulty is the implication that the study of Christianity is more important and relevant than the study of Islām. It is our belief that for a Muslim child this is manifestly unfair. **Whilst appreciating the need to understand and respect other faiths, it is wrong for a curriculum to suggest that other religions are subordinate to Christianity. Indeed, it would be very damaging for children to grow up believing that to be really British and contribute meaningfully to society, a Christian background is almost essential.**

As with Collective Worship, parents have a legal right to withdraw their children from RE lessons (Education Act 1996, Section 389(1)(a)(b)(c) and if such a request is made by a parent, **then the school must comply.** *(Circular 1/94 on RE and CW, paras. 46,47)* If Muslim parents withdraw their children from RE there are two options open to them:

1. The Muslim children may be withdrawn from RE and given alternative work or study to do, supervised by a member of staff.

2. If a suitably-qualified Muslim teacher is available (even from outside the school), the 1996 Education Act (Section 389(6)) allows children who have been withdrawn from RE to receive religious studies lessons within the school, as long as this is at no extra cost to the school. If arranged in an atmosphere of mutual respect, such arrangements could help to cement a relationship of understanding and cooperation between the school and Muslim parents.

Muslim pupils should be encouraged to study **Islām at GCSE level,** either as a subject in its own right developed by the **University of London Examinations and Assessment Council (ULEAC),** now called **Edexcel** in close consultation with the MET. It is available from **Edexcel. (Religious Studies (Islām), 190 High Holborn, London WC1V 7BH, Tel: 0870 240 9800 Fax: 020 7190 5700).**

The following chart shows the number of candidates who have taken GCSE Religious (Islām) since 1993.

## Candidates entering for GCSE Islām 1993 - 2003

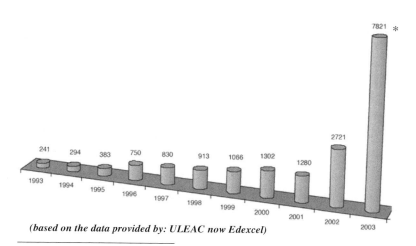

*(based on the data provided by: ULEAC now Edexcel)*

---

*\* The figures for 2003 are for 5 units on Islām, and others for units A and B upto 2002.* **13**

The introduction of such a course of study and similar initiatives which cater for the needs of Muslim pupils can make a substantial contribution towards the establishment of sound and positive relations between school, home and community. Such efforts might counteract the belief held by many Muslims that the education system is not supportive of their aspirations. RE teachers would find that giving Muslim pupils the opportunity to take a Religious Studies GCSE in Islām would generate greater motivation and enthusiasm, with an obviously stronger possibility of better examination results.

### SEX AND RELATIONSHIP EDUCATION (SRE) IN SCHOOLS

Allāh has made natural arrangements for humans to learn about their sexuality as they grow and develop but young people are in need of knowledge and understanding to cope with real-life situations. The subject of sex was not a taboo amongst early Muslim scholars and they gave specific information and guidance on reproduction, menstruation, childbirth and marriage. There are also clear guidelines on sexual etiquette within marriage. Any sexual activity outside marriage is clearly forbidden.

> *O Mankind! If you have a doubt about the Resurrection,*
> *(consider) that We created you out of dust, then out of sperm,*
> *then out of a leech-like clot ['alaqah],*
> *then out of a morsel of flesh,*
> *partly formed and partly unformed...*
> *{Al-Qur'ān, chapter 22, verse 5}*

> *Proclaim! (or read!)*
> *in the name of thy Lord and Cherisher, Who created –*
> *Created man out of a (mere) leech-like clot ['alaq].*
> *{Al-Qur'ān, chapter 96, verses 1–2}*

Since there may be many sceptics who doubt the validity of using the Qur'ānic text as a teaching aid in SRE it may be worthwhile to know that the word 'alaq, which is translated in the above verses as 'a leech-like clot', contains within it the meaning that this is 'something which clings'. It is now known, after 1400 years of the revelation of the Qur'ān, that the fertilised egg literally clings to the wall of the mother's womb!

Although parents usually find it difficult to talk about sex with their children (and surveys have shown that parents shy away from this), they are in most cases the right people to deal with this delicate and important topic. **The law of England and Wales places sex education on the curriculum in every maintained secondary school under section 2 of the Education Reform Act 1988 (as amended by section 241(1) of the Education Act 1993), and at the discretion of school governors in all maintained primary schools under section 18(2) of the Education (No 2) Act 1986.**

Muslims must look for ways to ensure their children receive responsible sex education based on the values of family life and morality. Both Muslim and non-Muslim parents should work towards a sex education programme that promotes sexual relations only within the framework of marriage, emphasizing the value of family life, morality and decency, focussing on the dangers of extramarital sexual relationships devoid of any responsibility and accountability. Within an Islāmic context such values and code of conduct do not change with time and place. Muslims must work towards the full recognition of their religious needs by those in authority, when in a non-Muslim country or environment.

A responsible, happy and contented society should be the aim of all, rather than a society that struggles with problems resulting from unbridled liberal and permissive sexual behaviour.

## THE CONTENT OF SEX AND RELATIONSHIP EDUCATION (SRE)

In Islām, marriage is the only basis for family life and sexual relationship, in contrast to the society in which we live, where extramarital sex is not only tolerated but has become the norm. Muslims, therefore, should urge schools to make sure the sex education they provide is given '...with due regard to moral considerations and the value of family life.' [*Education (No 2) Act 1986, Section 46*]

Sex and Relationship Education (SRE) is about learning about sex, sexuality, feelings, relationships, sex-related disease, abortion, contraception and physical aspects of reproduction (as a part of the National Science Curriculum).

**Moral considerations and the value of family life do form part of SRE but the inclusion of 'relationships' outside marriage has**

**undermined the importance of marriage and family life. The Civil Partnership Bill, 2004 (now being debated in the parliament) allowing registration of civil partnerships between same sex couples will undermine the importance of marriage (between a man and women) and family life even further.**

All schools must prepare a separate written statement of their policy with regard to the provision of SRE, and must make copies available free of charge to parents of any child registered at the school if they ask for one [Education Act 1993, section 241(5)]. Further, schools must publish in their prospectus a summary of the content and organisation of any sex education they provide [*Education (Schools Information) Regulations 1993; sec371 (3 a–b), Education Act, 1996*]

The DfEE (Department for Education and Employment) Circular 0116/2000 – Sex and Relationship Education Guidance, which replaced Circular 5/94 Education Act 1993: Sex Education in schools, gives important advice about what is expected of school sex education. Muslim, and indeed many non-Muslim, parents would note that it addresses some of their concerns about this subject. The teaching of sex education and its policies should be developed in such a way that they, "...reflect the parents' wishes and the community they serve." [*Circular 0116/2000, paragraph 8, page 4*]

Circular 0116/2000 says that sex education "is lifelong learning about physical, moral and emotional development. It is about the understanding of the importance of marriage for family life, '*stable and loving relationships,*' respect, love and care. It is also about the teaching of sex, sexuality, and sexual health. It is not about the promotion of sexual orientation or sexual activity – this would be inappropriate teaching." [emphasis ours] [*Circular 0116/2000, paragraph 9, page 5*]

**Muslim and many non-Muslim parents will be upset to note that under the guise of 'stable and loving relationships' the importance and value of family life has been undermined by this Circular, which was not the case with the Circular 5/94.**

This Circular gives specific guidelines on sex education in primary schools. These are:

**"The Department recommends that all primary schools should**

have a sex and relationship education programme tailored to the age and the physical and emotional maturity of the children. It should ensure that both boys and girls know about puberty and how a baby is born – as set out in Key Stages 1 and 2 of the National Science Curriculum. Section 3 gives further information on what should be taught at these stages and how this should be rooted in the PSHE (Personal, social and health education) framework." [*Circular 0116/ 2000, paragraph 1.12, page 9*]

"All children, including those who develop earlier than the average, need to know about puberty before they experience the onset of physical changes. In the early primary school years, education about relationships needs to focus on friendship, bullying and the building of self-esteem." [*Circular 0116/2000, paragraph 1.13, page 9*]

"Meeting these objectives will require a graduated, age-appropriate programme of sex and relationship education. Teaching methods need to take account of the developmental differences of children and the potential for discussion on a one-to-one basis or in small groups. Schools should set a framework for establishing what is appropriate and inappropriate in a whole-class setting. Teachers may require support and training in answering questions that are better not dealt with in front of a whole class." [*Circular 0116/2000, paragraph 1.14, page 9*]

"It is important that the transition year before moving to secondary schools supports pupils' ongoing emotional and physical development effectively. As well as consulting parents more generally about the school's overall policy, primary schools should consult with parents before the transition year about the detailed content of what will be taught. This process should include offering parents support in talking to their children about sex and relationship education and how to link this with what is being taught in school." [*Circular 0116/2000, paragraph 1.15, page 9–10*]

"Schools should have clear parameters on what children will be taught in the transition year before moving to secondary school. This should include:

- changes in the body related to puberty, such as periods and voice breaking;
- when these changes are likely to happen and what issues may cause young people anxiety and how they can deal with these; and
- how a baby is conceived and born." [Circular 0116/2000, paragraph 1.16, page 10]

**On the use of materials the Circular mentions:**

**"The teaching of some aspects of sex and relationship education might be of concern to teachers and parents. Sensitive issues should be covered by the school's policy and in consultation with parents. Schools of a particular religious ethos may choose to reflect that in their sex and relationship education policy. Research demonstrates that good, comprehensive sex and relationship education does not make young people more likely to enter into sexual activity. Indeed it can help them learn the reasons for, and the benefits to be gained from, delaying such activity."** [*Circular 0116/2000, paragraph 1.7, page 8*]

**"Materials used in schools must be in accordance with the PSHE (Personal, Social and Health Education) framework and the law. Inappropriate images should not be used nor should explicit material not directly related to explanation. Schools should ensure that pupils are protected from teaching and materials which are inappropriate, having regard to the age and cultural background of the pupils concerned. Governors and head teachers should discuss with parents and take on board concerns raised, both on materials which are offered to schools and on sensitive material to be used in the classroom. The Department of Health will be issuing guidance to Health Authorities to make clear that any materials they develop for use in schools must be in line with this guidance. Schools will also want to ensure that children are protected from accessing unsuitable materials on the internet. The Department's "Superhighways Safety" information pack outlines ways that schools can make access to the Internet safe and prevent children from accessing unsuitable material."** [*Circular 0116/ 2000, paragraph 1.8, page 8*]

**The circular also mentions that the National Healthy School**

Standard (NHSS) introduced in 1999 includes specific themes on sex education:

"The National Healthy School Standard (NHSS) was introduced in October 1999 to support and complement the new PSHE framework. Sex and relationship education is one of a number of specific themes which make up the Standard. The NHSS has specific criteria which ensure that schools can confidently set the context and ethos for the effective delivery of sex and relationship education." [*Circular 0116/ 2000, paragraph 1.9, page 8–9*]

The Circular proposed to set a balance between the focus on physical aspects of reproduction and the discussion about feelings, relationships and values. While doing so, stable and loving relationships outside marriage have been mentioned. Muslims will obviously feel upset by this.

"Young people, when asked about their experiences of sex education at school, often complain about the focus on the physical aspects of reproduction and the lack of any meaningful discussion about feelings, relationships and values. Sex and relationship education set within the framework for PSHE across the four key stages will significantly redress that balance. It will help young people to respect themselves and others, and understand difference. Within the context of talking about relationships, children should be taught about the nature of marriage and its importance for family life and for bringing up children. The Government recognises that there are strong and mutually supportive relationships outside marriage. Therefore, children should learn the significance of marriage and stable relationships as key building blocks of community and society. Teaching in this area needs to be sensitive so as not to stigmatise children on the basis of their home circumstances." [*Circular 0116/ 2000, paragraph 1.21, page 11*]

Islām does not support the view of the government that there should be stable and supportive relationships outside marriage. Islām does not recognise any extra-marital relationships.

SRE should provide factual information objectively and educate young people to look forward to adult life with a sense of responsibility, accountabilty, happiness and building a strong, stable family life. Objective discussion based on clear and accurate information on all forms of sexuality could be useful depending on how these discussions are conducted. Muslim parents will be reassured if during SRE the Islāmic viewpoint is properly discussed.

## ADVICE TO SCHOOLS AND GOVERNORS

Schools and their governors should consider sensitively and objectively the Islāmic Perspective on SRE and this should form a part of school sex education programmes. The role of the Muslim governors of a school is important in this respect. They should consult Muslim parents and represent their views in discussions about the SRE programme of the school.

Head teachers should consult the Imāms of the local mosques and Muslim organisations when they receive representation from Muslim parents on any aspect of SRE.

Requests from Muslim parents should be dealt with carefully and sensitively using professional expertise and empathy. Some Muslim parents have strong views on aspects of SRE and these should be tactfully and sensitively dealt with.

Circular 0116/2000 on SRE deals with the concerns of parents in sections 5.5 to 5.7 on page 26. These are:

"The role of parents as sex educators is emphasised in the Home Office strategy, "Supporting Families", as is their need for support from professionals. The Teenage Pregnancy report also recommends that parents are given more help to talk to their children about sex and relationships. National and local media campaigns will target parents. Each local authority area has a co-ordinator who will encourage schools to identify and develop effective approaches of supporting parents." [*Circular 0116/2000, paragraph 5.5, page 26*]

"Schools should always work in partnership with parents, consulting them regularly on the content of sex and relationship education programmes. Reflection around parents' own experiences of sex education can often lead to a productive discussion in which teachers and parents can start planning sex and relationship education provision for their children. Parents need to know that the school's sex and relationship education programme will complement and support their role as parents and that they can be actively involved in the determination of the school's policy." [*Circular 0116/2000, paragraph 5.6, page 26*]

"Parents have the right to withdraw their children from all or part of the sex and relationship education provided at school except for those parts included in the statutory National Curriculum (see section 3). Schools should make alternative arrangements in such cases. The DfEE will offer schools a standard pack of information for parents who withdraw their children from sex and relationship education." [*Circular 0116/2000, paragraph 5.7, page 26*]

"When schools publish details of their SRE programme, they should bear in mind that some parents whose first language is not English may need to have translations of the school's policy. Schools should ensure that parents understand the right of withdrawal and how to exercise it." [Paragraph 0116/2000]. If aspects of SRE occur in other areas of the curriculum (excepting those parts in the statutory National Curriculum) parents should be informed. Schools would benefit from an exercise which identifies all those areas of the curriculum where SRE issues may arise. Parents should be made aware of these areas of the curriculum.

It would be wrong and unfair for schools to put any pressure on parents who decide to exercise the right of withdrawal. There have been many instances where teachers or head teachers have put great pressure on parents who wanted to withdraw their children from SRE. The Muslim Educational Trust has dealt with a number of cases where the attitude of the school authorities (head teacher and governors) was less than helpful in solving the legitimate concerns of Muslim parents, many of whom admittedly are not as well acquainted with education laws and not as articulate as the authorities. In our opinion, all such problems are not difficult to solve given understanding, empathy, goodwill and a common concern to help the child grow up responsibly towards adult life in the society in which he/she lives.

Goodwill and understanding are essential if problems are to be resolved in a manner acceptable to all and there should be an amicable way of looking at the problems arising out of sex education. Preconceived ideas and a lack of knowledge producing ill-founded fears on both sides should not be used as excuses for closing the doors of consultation. Long-cherished beliefs and values should be respected and the authorities should deal sensitively and professionally with difficulties faced by Muslims in all aspects of life, including sex education.

## ADVICE TO MUSLIM PARENTS

The basic responsibility for passing faith and heritage to young children rests largely with parents, who should set a good example for their children. If they set a bad example, it makes it harder for those children to discover the true standards of Islām for themselves, and the beauty of being born to a Muslim family may be lost. Young Muslims must deal with a multi-faith, multicultural society and try to carve their own niche outside the home. If parents set them good examples then it is reasonable to hope that they will try to emulate their elders and, in turn, set a good example for their own children in the future.

As we have said, parents should ideally be able to give their children advice on sexual matters in accordance with the teachings of Islām. However, many parents may not feel comfortable doing this. Nevertheless, it is the parental duty to ensure that children receive both correct information and protection from immorality. Many parents, both Muslim and non-Muslim, consider discussion about sex with their children a taboo. It might be possible for parents to arrange with a local mosque or madrasah for their children to receive Islāmic instruction on these matters from someone more expert or knowledgeable on the subject. They must also make sure that their children have access to good sources of information, particularly Islāmic sources. Muslim parents should keep in mind that Allāh, the Creator, has given guidance in the Qur'ān on matters like procreation, the reproduction process, menstruation, childbirth and marital relationships. Prophet Muḥammad ﷺ gave many guidelines on human sexuality, so parents should not shy away from discussing these matters with their own children, whose welfare is of utmost importance to them. If parents do shy away from their responsibilities, children may learn the wrong things from peers, from the media, from inappropriate sex education materials, or from sexually explicit magazines, books, videos and internet.

Schools should make the SRE policy available to parents who ask. It is very important that parents make every effort to find out what is taught in their children's school, and what materials are used for this purpose. If there are other Muslim and non-Muslim parents at the school sharing these concerns, they may find it easier to work together. Working with people of other faiths for a common good or truth is in accordance with the prophetic example. SRE may not always be delivered as a separate subject. Where it occurs in the National Curriculum Science Order, which is restricted to purely biological aspects, there is no right of withdrawal. But sex education may arise in other areas, such as PSHE, English, Drama, Citizenship and so on. Parents should make sure that if this happens, it is with their full knowledge and consent.

Parents (Muslims and non-Muslims) should be aware that some of the material prepared for sex education lessons is produced by outside agencies whose objectives may not be the same as theirs. All the resources to be used by the school should be scrutinised in detail by Muslim parents before they agree to it being given or shown to their children. This includes books, videos, leaflets, work sheets, and any other material to be used. **It is preferable if parents and the school work together to develop a SRE policy that meets both the legal and Islāmic requirements. When this is not possible, which is sometimes the case, parents will then have to exercise the legal right to withdraw their children from the SRE programme, without any fear or duress.**

Parents should make sure that the SRE curriculum follows the advice given in the Circular 0116/2000. Furthermore, the curriculum should warn against aspects of this permissive society, where sex outside of marriage is not considered sinful by many, rather is accepted as a norm. Pupils should be informed that no contraceptive method – apart from abstinence – is 100% safe (e.g. they should be told that out of 733 women who had abortions in one British city between September 1988 and March 1989, 334 reported that their partners used condoms for contraceptive 'protection'

[Source: The British Journal of Family Planning, 1990, 15:112-117]); that there are dangerous side-effects to 'The Pill'; that sexually transmitted diseases are dangerous and that abortion is forbidden except in exceptional circumstances. Details of the emotional effects of early sexual intercourse should also be prominent in SRE.

If children are in a mixed-sex school, parents should ask for single-sex lessons on sex education to be arranged, especially on matters such as contraception, as this will ensure the confident participation of all pupils, something that may not always be forthcoming in mixed-sex classes.

Muslim parents' efforts should be directed towards ensuring that the sex education programme at their children's school is not against the basic teachings of their faith. Ultimately, if the school does not produce an acceptable sex education programme, parents have the right to withdraw their children from all or part of it [Section 17A of the Education Reform Act 1988 (inserted by section 241(2) of the Education Act 1993)]. Parents do not have to give reasons for their decision nor do they have to indicate what other arrangements they intend to make for providing sex education for their children. But it is preferable to discuss with the head teacher of the school and explain the religious reasons for exercising the legal right of withdrawal.

### ADVICE TO MUSLIM ORGANISATIONS

Muslim organisations also have the responsibility to help young Muslims grow towards a healthy Islāmic identity. Combined effort from parents and organisations is essential to achieve the desired educational objectives for the benefit of Muslim children in non-Muslim schools. We must act in a concerted and coordinated way to persuade and impress upon those responsible for the education of our children about our particular religious needs. Given a logical, persuasive and articulate approach, most of the educational concerns could be amicably resolved. Of course, there will be circumstances and situations which would need very careful handling on the part of the authorities and Muslims. However, accommodation and understanding of diverse views are not unattainable. We must work towards this. Individual parents may find it difficult to affect change in their schools.

But when local mosques and Muslim organisations work in a concerted way, schools could be persuaded to devise a SRE programme which would be acceptable to Muslim pupils and parents.

It may be difficult for some schools to obtain accurate information about Islām and the needs of Muslim pupils. Whereas organisations like the Muslim Educational Trust and a number of other national organisations could give help on a national level, local mosques and organisations are ideally placed to ensure that schools in their communities respect the religious requirements of their Muslim pupils.

## ADVICE TO MUSLIM PUPILS

As a Muslim pupil you should remember that you are required by your religion to grow up as a responsible human being (Khalīfah – the agent of Allāh on earth) in any society where you live. You must not forget that your duty is to learn and educate yourself to carry out your responsibilities in adult life purposefully and efficiently. You must not be carried away by the 'trendy' ideas which eventually may prove disastrous for you. Remember that as an example of behaviour you have the best of mankind in the Prophet Muḥammad ﷺ, who was a 'Mercy to the Worlds'. We should emulate his example for our success in this life and the life after death. The criterion of what is right and wrong is based on what Allāh revealed to Prophet Muḥammad ﷺ, which is the Qur'ān and the example of Prophet Muḥammad ﷺ. If we follow our own desires we might go astray. Allāh says :

> *... And who is more astray than he who follows his own likes and dislikes without any guidance from Allāh. Surely Allāh guides not the wrongdoers.*

> {*Al-Qur'ān, chapter 28, verse 50*}

> *... perhaps you hate a thing and it is good for you; and perhaps you love a thing and it is bad for you.*

> {*Al-Qur'ān, chapter 2, verse 216*}

It is in this context you should know that it is your right to have correct information about sexual matters in accordance with the teachings of Islām.

Sex is an integral part of human life and therefore you should not feel shy to ask questions to your parents, whose main concern is your welfare, success and prosperity. However, if it is difficult to discuss the subject with your parents, you should try to find a knowledgeable, practising Muslim who can answer your questions. This may be a local Imām or Islāmic Studies teacher, a knowledgeable community leader, or an approachable and knowledgeable relative. **You should also try to read reliable books (such as those printed in bold in the Appendix III). You can also write to Islāmic organisations for advice and information.**

There are many non-Muslim organisations who advise on matters of SRE. Some of these have an attitude to life that does not fit with the beliefs and teachings of Islām. It is important, then, that you treat information from such organisations with care and caution.

The great majority of teachers will have a keen interest in your welfare, and will want to be able to give you advice should you need it. You should make sure that this advice does not in any way go against your beliefs as a Muslim. You should tell your parents if any books, videos or other materials used for sex education are in any way offensive or embarrassing, so that they can be checked to make sure they are not against Islāmic teachings. Never try to hide things from your parents; feel confident to talk to your parents and do not feel embarrassed. Remember, this affects your life and it is very important that you should tell your parents what you are taught as a part of SRE in your schools.

The Internet has its enormous benefits but it is not without dangers. It would be to your benefit and welfare not to be induced to go into unethical and unislāmic sites which would lead to disastrous consequences which have been highlighted in the media. Always remember: our Loving and Merciful Creator knows every aspect of our life, we cannot hide anything from Him. This consciousness of Allāh (Taqwā) is the key to our success in this world and in the Ākhirah.

Homosexual practices are not allowed in Islām; they incur the anger of Allāh, and are severely punished in an Islāmic society. Schools should not promote homosexuality. If there are teachers or pupils in your school who are homosexual, that is their business, and you should leave them alone.

Islām does not approve of free mixing between sexes. If you are in a mixed sex school, try to restrict your friendships to your own sex; do not seek to be alone with pupils of the opposite sex. Boyfriend-girlfriend relationships inevitably lead to problems, and mean going against the teachings of Islām. Remember, these teachings are designed for your own benefit and welfare.We pray that you adhere to these teachings and gain success in this life and the Hereafter. *(Source: Sex Education: The Muslim Perspective - Ghulam Sarwar, 2004)*

## PHYSICAL EDUCATION (PE)

Physical Education is a compulsory part of the National Curriculum at every key stage, and covers six areas of activity:

- athletic activities
- dance
- games
- gymnastic activities
- outdoor and adventurous activities
- swimming

At Key Stages 1 and 2 pupils must experience all six areas of activity. At Key Stage 3 pupils pursue at least four areas of activity, whilst at Key Stage 4 pupils are required to take only two activities from either one or two areas.

Prophet Muhammad ﷺ encouraged physical exercise and sports, and particularly commended swimming, archery and horse-riding. As with any activity, though, there are basic Islāmic requirements which must be satisfied, such as prohibitions on indecent clothing and free-mixing between the sexes.

Once children reach the age of puberty they must follow the Islāmic requirements relating to dress: boys must be covered at least from the knee to the navel; for girls, only the face and the hands should remain uncovered (when in the presence of men whom, according to Islāmic law, they could marry). At all ages (even before puberty), children must not expose their private parts in front of each other, and they will often dress with the modesty of adults. Clothing should not be revealing or skin-tight. Muslim children should, therefore, be allowed to wear sportswear compatible with the Islāmic dress code.

It is expressly forbidden for Muslim boys and girls to be in a state of undress in front of anyone else, even of their own sex. Where changing rooms do not have private cubicles, Muslim children could use a large towel or a sarong whilst changing to preserve their modesty. A non-Muslim should not be naked in front of a Muslim.

Complete nudity in public is forbidden in Islām and is abhorrent to Muslims. Where shower facilities are communal, a Muslim child must not be forced to bathe naked. **We suggest that using Bermuda shorts or three-quarter length tracksuit trousers or something similar will suffice while showering.** However, even dressed as such, they should not shower communally when others are naked. An alternative arrangement would be for Muslim boys and girls to delay their shower until they reach home. An increasing number of schools permit this, and have found that it poses no hazard to health.

The psychological effect of enforced communal nudity is damaging; this view is shared by non-Muslims and Muslims alike. In an article in *The Guardian* (The bare facts, 24 June 1986), Robert Wilkins, a Consultant Child and Adolescent Psychiatrist, wrote: "Compulsory group nakedness constitutes a gross infringement upon the civil liberties of a child and is a prospect no adult would willingly contemplate ... It is difficult to explain why such ceremonials are allowed to continue when other dehumanising rituals such as corporal punishment have all but ceased."

Going on to explain that his dislike for sports activities was induced by a "loathing" for communal showers and "the profound indignity of being naked in the company of strangers", Dr. Wilkins claims that "it is hard enough to bear the misery of visible impediments, but to be made to parade naked and reveal hitherto hidden inadequacies is the quintessential humiliation for the pubescent child."

It was noted in the same article that "many schools, especially girls' schools, are quietly dropping the requirement for children to shower after games and PE and have found that no dire epidemics or health hazards have occurred as a result of stale bodies. Other schools are attempting to reschedule PE to the last period of the day, allowing children to shower in the privacy of their own homes." Such moves have, according to some teachers, provoked a noticeable increase in the interest shown by children in sport which, surely, is the purpose of PE in the first place.

**It is always preferable for Muslim children, once they have reached puberty, to have single-sex lessons. This becomes an absolute necessity in the case of swimming.** It is not just the group which must be of one sex; the whole session at the swimming pool should be single-sex, with instructors and lifeguards of the same sex as the swimmers. Most public swimming baths have women-only sessions, but it is very rare that one finds men-only sessions. If schools are unable to make arrangements for single-sex swimming, then Muslim pupils should be excused from attending.

We quote here from the **Swimming Charter** published by DfES in December 2003 under the heading **Ethnic Minority Groups:**

**The Swimming Advisory Group's report highlighted the fact that many children from ethnic communities were failing to reach the minimum Key Stage 2 target.**

**This is particularly true for children of Islāmic faith background whose parents may object on grounds of modesty and decency. Muslim girls in particular may exhibit reluctance to swimming in mixed classes with boys. Making alternative arrangments such as all male and all female classes can often solve these issues. Schools, local authorities (including LEAs) and pool managers should work together to remove unnecessary barriers to learning. They should consider block booking separate classes for girls and boys (either from a number of schools or with different age groups from the same school), using same sex teachers for classes, if appropriate, and adopt flexible clothing codes.** [*Document ref PE/SC (December, 2003)*]

**Although it is one of the activities listed under PE, it is our view that dance has no academic significance or value, nor does it contribute positively to meaningful human knowledge.** Islām, as an all-embracing way of life, has specific limits on certain topics; these include a modest dress code, the prohibition of many types of music (see section on Music), the means to prevent the arousal of the human being's base feelings outside

**29**

of marriage, and the prohibition of free-mixing of the sexes. Since most, if not all, forms of dance involve either some or all of the above and manage to contravene all of them at one time or another, it is clear to see that dance as is generally practised is not allowed for Muslims.

Sometimes schools find that they are unable to fulfil all of the requirements of Muslim children. In such circumstances head teachers should exempt their Muslim pupils from those areas where they cannot meet Islāmic requirements. It is our experience that schools where head teachers respond positively in such situations provide more harmonious and balanced learning environments.

## ART

Children must study art at key stages one, two and three. The National Curriculum does not require the study of art at Key Stage 4.

Islām does not prohibit the study of any meaningful and useful area of human knowledge, but there are certain ground-rules to be followed. Indeed, Islām encourages the study of art, and has made an enormous contribution to art and architecture over the centuries; but those aspects of art which involve human images and iconography are specifically prohibited. Ideally, a school's art curriculum should include a study of Islāmic art and architecture, making it possible for Muslim pupils to realise their full potential in this field.

There is no reason – at any key stage – why Muslim pupils should be made to contravene the guiding principles of Islām in their study of art.

## MUSIC

Whenever someone sets out to study a particular subject, they must first ascertain whether or not it is something which will contribute positively to their knowledge. In Islām, this means whether the subject will make the student more aware of their Creator and their role in life, or if it will divert them from the remembrance of Allāh and the Guidance He has given to mankind through His final prophet, Muḥammad ﷺ.

It is unfortunate that, by incorporating Music in the National Curriculum, the needs and concerns of Muslim pupils have been entirely ignored. Music must be studied at each of the first three key stages, and is optional at Key

Stage 4. Schools with Muslim pupils may find that their parents offer apparently conflicting advice, thoughts and beliefs on the subject of music. Some parents will think that it is perfectly in order for their children to study music in school; some will be happy with certain aspects of the subject but unhappy with others; some will be completely unhappy that their children are forcibly exposed to what they consider to be a *harām* (forbidden) activity. The matter largely depends on the degree of practice of the faith within the home and the amount of interest that the parents take in what their children are studying at school.

Is music *halāl* (permissible) or *harām* (forbidden)? In the most famous collection of the Prophet's sayings (*Ahadith*), the Prophet ﷺ is reported to have said,

> "There will be [at some future time] people from my Ummah [nation] who will seek to make lawful fornication, the wearing of silk [for men], wine-drinking and the use of musical instruments ..."

*(Ṣaḥīḥ Al-Bukhāri (The Book of Drinks, chapter 6)*

The fact that the Prophet ﷺ said "... will seek to make lawful ... the use of musical instruments ..." makes it clear that their use is, in fact, unlawful. The word translated as 'musical instruments' (ma'āzif) has been clearly established – according to the correct Arabic usage – to mean (a) musical instruments, (b) the sounds of those musical instruments, and (c) singing to musical accompaniment.

According to the majority of Islāmic scholars, then, the use of musical instruments generally is not allowed. The fact that there are quite a few famous Muslim musicians who do not follow Islāmic guidance on this matter, and that many Muslims listen to music which is prohibited in Islām, should not be used to 'prove' that it is in order for Muslim pupils to play musical instruments.

It is clear that the National Curriculum requirements for pupils to, for example, "perform pieces/accompaniments on a widening range of more sophisticated instruments ..." (Key Stage 2) will cause difficulties for some Muslims, as will the need to "listen attentively and respond to a widening range of music ..." (Key Stage 2) which, by Key Stage 3, will include "oratorio", a specifically Christianity-based type of music.

It is (incorrectly) argued that listening to and studying what is generally called "classical" music (i.e. music for full or chamber orchestra, or ensembles made up of instrumentalists from such groups) is not contrary to Islāmic teachings. However, the need to discuss works such as, for example, the overture Romeo and Juliet by Tchaikovsky or any one of a number of "boy meets girl" operas (e.g. Bizet's Carmen) inevitably introduces Muslim children to concepts which are alien to their beliefs (e.g. premarital intimacy). The inclusion of modern songs and styles of music will also almost certainly lead pupils into *harām* fields of study.

In order to "respond" to certain types of music it is suggested that pupils could "identify contrasts in ... Stravinsky's Firebird and describe these contrasts through art or dance." (Key Stage 3) This is a good example of how one undesirable act (listening to music) can lead on to others, it being almost certain that such efforts to "describe these contrasts" will involve pupils in drawing animate objects (forbidden in Islām) and dancing, possibly in mixed-sex groups (forbidden for pupils beyond puberty, which is when they would be expected to reach such a stage of musical study).

Given that much of the National Curriculum aims at encouraging pupils to play musical instruments, Muslim children will clearly be disadvantaged. They are being asked to do something which their religion prohibits them from doing. Since the emphasis in the curriculum is on musical performance using instruments and the study of well-known pieces of music, it appears to be impossible to simply allow Muslim children to study musical theory in relation to the human voice and perform unaccompanied songs of an Islāmic nature (in praise of Allāh, marvelling at His creation, etc.). The National Curriculum simply does not offer any such leeway for accommodating the religious beliefs of pupils who will, in some schools, be the vast majority on roll.

It may be that the aims of the curriculum are actually too complicated for hard-pressed schools to put into practice, and that they will be quietly ignored. If not, we cannot see how schools and Muslim parents will cope. However, it is hoped that the above guidance will, at least, offer some help to those who have the difficult task of trying to balance their legal obligations to follow the National Curriculum with educating children **in accordance with the wishes of the parents.** (Education Act, 1996, Section 9) Requests from Muslim parents for their children to be exempted from the study of music should thus not be dismissed out of hand; forcing children to participate without regard to their religious beliefs could only be viewed as the imposition of 'cultural superiority'. It is to be hoped that schools will respect the Islāmic concerns of Muslim parents and children in this matter.

A commonly-held belief is that Islām is against expressions of the joys of life in artistic forms, but this is not the case. On the contrary, the regulations of Islām in these matters are designed to allow such expressions whilst at the same time closing the loopholes through which totally free expression can lead to immoral acts and the corruption of society.

## School Uniform

Muslim children should be allowed to follow the Islāmic dress code, with the colours of the school uniform in mind, if necessary.

Islām requires boys and girls to conform at all times to the dress regulations outlined in the Qur'ān and the Sunnah (the example of Prophet Muḥammad, peace and blessings be upon him), which hold that modesty is the uppermost concern. After puberty, girls' dress may include loose, baggy trousers, long skirts reaching to the ankles or any other appropriate dress which is neither tight-fitting nor transparent. The whole body – except the hands and the face – should be covered. A headcovering (ḥijāb, which could also be in the school colours) is also required, sufficient to ensure that the hair is not visible. There have been some instances where Muslim girls who have taken to wearing the ḥijāb have been sent home and banned from following the requirements of their faith. Two arguments are usually used: 1. Other Muslim girls – even from the same family – do not wear ḥijāb so why should these girls? 2. A scarf or suchlike is a safety hazard in school laboratories.

Both arguments are easily refuted: Just because one person chooses not to practice or follow their faith, that is no reason to prevent others from doing so. The majority of people in Britain who would call themselves

**33**

Christians do not attend church regularly; is that a reason to prevent those who do from doing so? Of course not! As for the safety excuse, it is an accepted fact that many people in industry, for various reasons, wear hair nets or otherwise keep their hair tied back so that it does not get caught in machinery, fall into food, etc. There is no reason why a suitably-tied ḥijāb cannot fulfil the same purpose; indeed, it is actually safer than allowing girls' hair to hang loose in the laboratory.

The guidelines concerning dress, inasmuch as clothes should be neither tight-fitting nor transparent, also apply to boys who have reached the age of puberty. Again, they should be allowed to wear loose-fitting clothes in any school colours necessary to fulfil their Islāmic obligations.

Guidelines published on TeacherNet developed by DfES on school uniform has a welcome paragraph on **Cultural, race and religious requirements** which we reproduce bellow:

**Whilst pupils must adhere to a school's uniform policy, schools must be sensitive to the needs of different cultures, races and religions. The DfES expects schools to accommodate these needs, within a general uniform policy. For example, allowing Muslim girls to wear appropriate dress and Sikh boys to wear traditional headdress.**

**The DfES does not consider it appropriate that any pupil should be disciplined for non-compliance with a school uniform policy, which results from them having to adhere to a particular cultural, race or religious dress code.** *(Source: http://www.teachernet.gov.uk/management/ atoz/u/uniform).*

This guidance, if acted upon, will go a long way to address the concerns of Muslim parents about school uniform. **Recently Islamic dress for girls became an issue in Tower Hamlet Schools** *(Source: The Sunday Times, 7 Nov. 2004 page 7).* Headteachers, Mosque leaders, LEA and Council representatives met to discuss the issue and decided to allow Muslim girls to wear Islamic dress. This shows how with understanding and consultation, the needs of Muslim pupils could be met.

**Finally, one aspect which is raised every now and again is that of Muslim boys keeping a beard, following the Sunnah of Prophet Muḥammad** ﷺ. Schools seem to have no problem in allowing Sikh boys to have beards, presumably because any attempt to force them to shave could be prosecuted under race relations legislation. Muslims, however, have no such legal protection. *The arguments used against Muslims in this respect apply equally to Sikhs so there can be no reasonable grounds for allowing one group to keep beards while prohibiting the other.* To keep a beard is the most natural way to follow the Sunnah; schools should not discourage pupils who choose to practice their faith in this way.

## PROVISION FOR MUSLIM PRAYERS

From the age of ten, every Muslim must pray five times a day at fixed times:

| | |
|---|---|
| *Fajr* | between dawn and sunrise |
| *Zuhr* | between midday and mid-afternoon |
| *'Asr* | between mid-afternoon and sunset |
| *Maghrib* | just after sunset |
| *'Ishā'* | between nightfall and daybreak |

Some of these prayers (depending on the length of the day as the seasons change) will fall within the school day, usually during the lunch and afternoon breaks. The obligatory portion of each prayer will usually last ten minutes at the most. Head teachers are requested to provide the facilities (i.e. a place for ritual ablution – wudu – and a prayer room) for those Muslim pupils who ask for them.

Whilst the daily prayers can be said virtually anywhere, the midday prayer on Fridays – Ṣalātul Jumu'ah – must be said in congregation by men and boys, preferably in the largest mosque possible. Hence, some parents may ask for their boys to be withdrawn from school, normally during the lunch break in order to attend Ṣalātul Jumu'ah in the local mosque. Such requests should be granted whenever possible unless alternative arrangements can be made for the prayer to be conducted in the school by a suitably qualified person (an Imām) who is acceptable to and approved by the local Muslim community.

## HOLIDAYS AND RELIGIOUS FESTIVALS

Muslims generally celebrate two major festivals annually: 'Īdul Fiṭr and 'Īdul Aᵭhā. Both fall on dates calculated using the lunar calendar (in which the sighting of the new moon signals the start of every Islāmic month) and so the days move through the seasons year by year. In 2004, 'Īdul Fiṭr fell on the 13/14th November and 'Īdul A∂ḥā will be on the 21st-23rd January 2005 (the latter is a four-day celebration).

'Īdul Fiṭr celebrates the ending of the fasting month of Rama∂ān; 'Īdul A∂ḥā commemorates the willingness of Prophet Ibrahim (Abraham) to sacrifice his then only son Ismā'īl (Ishmael – peace be upon them both) and takes place at the culmination of the Ḥajj (pilgrimage to Makkah). 'Īdul A∂ḥā is celebrated by Muslims all over the world, not only those on the Ḥajj.

Head teachers should allow Muslim children to be absent from school on these festival days in accordance with section 444 (3) (c) of the 1996 Education Act.

## SCHOOL MEALS

Food and drink have direct effects on our health which is why Islām allows the consumption of all wholesome things. The Qur'ān contains clear rules on this matter. Muslims must not eat pork in any form, nor any food products containing it. All other meat is allowed as long as the animal has been slaughtered by a Muslim, without pre-stunning, whilst invoking the name of Allāh. This is called ḥalāl meat. If an animal is not slaughtered in such a fashion, it is ḥarām (forbidden). This applies to the meat itself and all derivatives – lard, animal fats, animal rennet (used in cheese) and gelatine. The concept of ḥalāl (that which is permissible) and ḥarām (that which is forbidden) should be properly understood by those who deal with Muslim communities.

Some LEAs have already made the welcome move of providing ḥalāl food in school canteens. Those without such a valuable facility should make sure that Muslim children have a choice of vegetarian food (all the while ensuring that no animal by-products or alcoholic substances are used in the cooking, of course). All ingredients should be displayed clearly. Again, some LEAs are already doing this but, unfortunately, much of the good work is spoilt at the servery hatch by the use of the same utensils for ḥalāl/vegetarian food and non-ḥalāl food. Separate utensils should be used.

With just a little care and effort, this is quite feasible.

## SCHOOL GOVERNORS

The governors play an important part in the management of a school, especially if it is a foundation school. Legislation has substantially increased the role governors have to play in the management of school.

**The Governing Body of a school is responsible for:**

1. **appointment of teachers and staff including the head teacher.**
2. **overseeing the budget of the school.**
3. **setting and monitoring the school's aims and policies regarding behaviour, sex-education, health and safety and school uniform.**
4. **ensuring the National Curriculum is taught and standards of achievement are improved.**
5. **making sure that the school is providing for the needs of all its pupils.**
6. **the maintenance of the premises of the school.**
7. **the provision of spiritual, moral and cultural development of all pupils.**

Although they will almost certainly be in a minority on any board of governors, Muslim parents and educationists should get involved as both elected and co-opted governors (or even LEA representatives). It is exceptional for there to be a majority of Muslim governors, even in schools with a majority of Muslim pupils. As a result, it is often an uphill struggle for the concerns of the Muslim parents to be given a fair hearing.

The ethos of society at large is reflected in the structures and procedures adopted in the management and administration of the governing body and in other, more general, school activities (school fetes, PTA meetings, etc.). **Wine** is frequently served in mixed-sex functions; such functions tend to discourage and limit the participation of practising Muslim men and women.

The experience of one Muslim governor, published in *The Times Educational Supplement* (Token efforts, 13.10.89), shows the continuing need for governor training to include at least some basic knowledge of minority (or majority) faith beliefs and practices: "As I rather nervously entered the head's study ... the first thing the head offered me was a glass of sherry … such meetings are often fraught with anxieties … and recipes for social disaster ('Here, have a sherry Mr. Hewitt. Oops. Sorry!' 'This is Mr. Hewitt; he is a Muslim but you can still talk to him.')." Such situations are unhelpful and serve to discourage Muslims from becoming governors.

Even so, it is essential for Muslims to be part of the governing body and to air their concerns, contributing to the overall improvement of the education provided by the school. Muslim governors should not hesitate to express their views in governors' meetings, and not just on matters relating directly to Muslim pupils. They should participate in the deliberations of the board on all topics as full and active members. To do this effectively, it is vital that they become acquainted with education law and procedures. Governors' training sessions can be used to good effect for this purpose.

It should be possible for Muslim governors to have a more meaningful role in schools where Muslim pupils are in the majority. Sadly, even in schools with over 90% muslim pupils, the number of Muslim Governors in the Governing Body are few. Muslim parents should actively involve themselves with the running of their children's schools. This is their legal, moral, and religious duty. Muslims should come forward to serve their community as governors in the knowledge that they have a positive contribution to make.

## STANDING ADVISORY COUNCILS ON RELIGIOUS EDUCATION (SACREs) AND AGREED SYLLABUS CONFERENCES (ASCs)

It is important for Muslims to be active in matters relating to religious education and collective worship. They can do this through membership of and participation in their local SACRE. This body provides a forum for consultation, discussion and advice for people from all religious backgrounds (and of none) and even in areas with relatively few Muslim pupils the Muslim contribution on SACRE is important.

The membership structure of all SACREs is such that even if Muslims form a majority of people in the area covered by the SACRE, the Muslim representatives on SACRE must share just one vote with the non-Anglican

Christians and all other non-Christian faiths. Section 11(4) of the ERA deals with the composition of groups on SACREs, and to this has been added Section 255 of the 1993 Education Act which states that the number of representatives shall "reflect broadly the proportionate strength" of the faith group or denomination in the area. Far from giving them more say, however, this could effectively exclude sizeable but thinly-spread faith groups from many SACREs.

This situation was pointed out to the government by the MET during the consultation on the Government White Paper, Choice and Diversity ... , published in 1992. It was reiterated in the consultation on the DFE Draft Circular published in October 1993. The MET suggested that the composition of SACREs be altered to remove such anomalies.

Muslim parents and organisations should make every effort to ensure that the Islāmic position is explained clearly and this can only be achieved if, a) Muslim representatives actually attend meetings regularly and make positive contributions, and b) those representatives are practising, knowledgeable Muslims. LEAs, whose duty it is to appoint members of SACREs, must make sure that they appoint Muslims who represent their faith, not their ethnic or national background. The 1993 Education Act (Section 258) allows for the Secretary of State to direct SACRE and ASC meetings to be open to the public. It remains to be seen whether this will lead to more openness or the creation of schisms between and within religious denominations.

The law now requires all locally agreed RE syllabuses which predate the 1988 ERA to be reviewed, and all RE syllabuses to be reviewed every five years. To do this, the LEA will convene an Agreed Syllabus Conference (ASC), the membership of which may well be (but does not have to be) based on the local SACRE. All of the points mentioned regarding SACREs apply equally to ASCs.

All religious education in non-denominational schools maintained by the LEA (i.e. not grant-maintained schools) must be taught according to the locally agreed syllabus. It is vital, therefore, for the Muslim community to be represented by competent, practising Muslims who can make full and effective contributions to the drafting of the RE syllabus.

## MUSLIM TEACHERS AND STAFF

It is sad that even in schools with 90%+ Muslim pupils there are few, if any, Muslim head teachers, teachers or non-teaching staff. This is often explained away as being due to a shortage of suitably qualified people. What is not so often explained is that it may also be due to discriminatory recruitment procedures.

The desirability of appointing staff who have the appropriate qualifications, skills, knowledge and experience is not denied by anyone concerned about academic standards in schools. Indeed, when the government realised that there was a national shortage of Maths, Science and Technology teachers, a special case was made for positive action; colleges, universities and all the 'partners' in education – including industry – were exhorted to ensure that children would get the teachers they deserve through a planned long-term programme. Funding came from the government and included special incentive allowances.

It is reasonable, then, that similar positive action should be undertaken to increase the number of Muslim teachers – this could only add to the quality of educational provision. Unfortunately, such positive action is conspicuous by its absence when it comes to the shortage of Muslim teachers. Nothing plausible has been said or done over the last 20 years to redress this imbalance, apart from rhetorical pronouncements by politicians and leading educationalists.

Similar inaction can be identified in the structures of the institutions which govern the recruitment, selection and promotion processes. Political will and commitment are needed to redress the imbalance and increase the number of employees from the minorities in an area where there is clear under-representation.

Muslim parents and organisations should encourage young people to choose teaching as a career, stressing the importance of education in Islām and the position of esteem a teacher has. Careers advisers could also play a part in this process.

## SINGLE-SEX SCHOOLS

Girls generally perform better in all-girls' schools; examination statistics support such arguments. On this basis alone, there is a strong case for retaining existing single-sex schools and even expanding this shrinking sector of the education world. Muslim parents who agonise over schools for their children – particularly their daughters – have a restricted choice. In some areas, all such schools have been closed or merged, even though the need to keep single-sex schools open was recognised and recommended by the Swann Committee report *(Education for All, pages 511- 512,1985).*

Muslim parents are not alone in wanting single-sex schools. Alan Grigg, headmaster of the School of St. Mary and St. Anne in Staffordshire, wrote in *The Times* (Boys a brain-drain on most girls, September 4, 1989), "Some people say that as the world is mixed, educational establishments should be mixed. This over-simplification infers that … in the learning situation too mixed classes are better than single-sex. The evidence indicates that the contrary is correct; all-girl classes in Maths, Sciences, computing and classics result in higher achievement than for girls in mixed classes."

Tony Thomas, headmaster of Casterton School in Cumbria, which came top of the 1993 independent schools' GCSE league table, is a firm believer in single-sex education, his previous school being for boys: "I think girls are very ambitious and prepared to work hard. In a single-sex school they can do that without being constantly judged on their outward appearance." (*The Independent*, 16 September 1993)

The diminishing number of girls' schools in Britain prompted the founding of the Association for Maintained Girls' Schools, supported by Baroness Warnock. The founder of the association, the head of a girls' school in Essex, said at the time, "Girls are seen as a 'civilising' influence on boys [in mixed schools] … but what about the repression many of them [the girls] suffer in co-educational classes, with the more forceful male personalities dominating lessons?" (*TES*, 1 March 1991)

**In 2004, girls' schools topped the schools' GCSE league table of all schools, capturing 31 of the top 50 places. At A-level, 19 were girls' schools out of the top 50** *(Source: www.timesonline.co.uk/ section0,,3321,00.html).* Girls also do better in Maths and Science in both GCSE and A levels in single sex schools *(Source: The Sunday Times, 14 November, 2004, page 15, main section).*

A Pembrokeshire mixed school will organise single sex classes from September 2004 to improve performance of both sexes *(BBC News, Thursday 2nd September 2004)*.

There is ample academic, as well as religious, justification for single-sex schools. Muslim parents should voice their concerns on this issue to their local councillors and Members of Parliament.

## PARENTAL INVOLVEMENT IN CHOOSING OPTIONS

The National Curriculum ensures that all children take GCSEs in the core and a selection of foundation subjects. In addition, schools offer other examination courses and, increasingly, a range of vocational courses. The choice of optional examination subjects will have important consequences, particularly in the options open to students at post-sixteen level.

Muslim parents who cannot speak good English and are not well-versed in the working of schools and the British education system may not, as a result, be able to help their children make *informed* choices from the options available at the 13+ and 16+ levels. They also may not be properly counselled by the school in such matters.

It is vital for parents to be aware of the options their children have, and of the increasing range of courses and opportunities available on completing compulsory education (i.e. at the age of sixteen). Head teachers are urged to involve Muslim parents fully in these choices, even if it means arranging for interpreters to be available for better communication between school and home. Full use should be made of the services of Careers Officers. Parents themselves should take an active interest and not simply ignore letters and invitations from the school on such matters. A lack of interest in the choice of options available in their children's education may have damaging consequences for their future career.

## MODERN FOREIGN LANGUAGES

The National Curriculum requires all children aged 11 - 16 (KS3 & KS4) to study a modern foreign language as one of their 'foundation subjects'. It is optional at Key Stages 1 & 2.

In most schools, children will be given a choice of European languages;

however, in schools with Muslim pupils it would be educationally sound to offer Arabic and the community languages among the modern language options. Such an option for Muslim children would combine greater access to their religious and cultural heritage with the benefits of wider linguistic skills and an enhanced sense of self-esteem and achievement.

Muslim parents should make their preference for Arabic and the community languages (Urdu, Bengali, Turkish, etc.) known to the school. The head teacher would then be in a position to assess the demand and make arrangements to offer the languages accordingly.

[The full list of modern foreign languages which count as National Curriculum languages is as follows: Arabic, Bengali, Chinese (Cantonese or Mandarin), Danish, Dutch, French, German, Modern Greek, Gujerati, Modern Hebrew, Hindi, Italian, Japanese, Portuguese, Punjabi, Russian, Spanish, Turkish and Urdu.]

## ISLĀMIC BOOKS IN THE SCHOOL LIBRARY

It is sad that many schools, even those with a majority of Muslim pupils, have very few – if any at all – *authentic* Islāmic books in stock, despite the fact that such books are now easily available in Britain. It is also sad that some schools stock books, presuming them to be on Islām, supplied free of charge by the non-Muslim Ahmadiyya/Qadiani group (who were formally declared by the world's Muslim scholars to be non-Muslims because of their refusal to accept the finality of prophethood in the person of Prophet Muḥammad ﷺ, an essential condition of the Islāmic faith).

Many teachers still appear to prefer and buy books on Islām written by non-Muslims, regardless of the authenticity and factual accuracy of the text. Schools with Muslim pupils should make an allowance within their budget to buy authentic Islāmic books for the school library and for classroom use. A list of selected books on Islām for teachers' and pupils' use is given in *Appendix III*. This may be used by school librarians and heads of department when selecting books for purchase. Schools should also use the resource pack produced by **Books for Schools Project** of **the Muslim Council of Britain** (MCB, Board House, 64 The Broadway, Stratford, London E15 1NT Tel: 020 8432 0586 Fax: 020 8432 0587).

## ENGLISH AS AN ADDITIONAL LANGUAGE (EAL) AND MULTICULTURAL STUDIES

Some Muslim children start school in Britain with little or no command of English, and are provided with special help by teaching and non-teaching staff; such staff are mainly called Language Support Teachers . In addition, some LEAs provide teachers to promote multiculturalism. In both cases, English-speaking, non-Muslim teachers without bilingual skills are nearly always appointed. Such a situation is both academically unsound and economically wasteful.

It would be appropriate to appoint teachers with bilingual or intercultural skills. This means that in schools with substantial numbers of Muslim children the appointment of the head teacher and other senior staff with suitable qualifications and having such skills, knowledge and experience is essential rather than just desirable. Section 11 funding was used for language support teaching, this is no longer available. A new scheme called **Ethnic Minority Achievement Grant** (EMAG) has been initiated by the DfES in 2002. Even if no additional funding is available, the needs of Muslim children should be catered for from within the school budget. Muslim parents may be willing to contribute to the funding of the teaching of EAL.

## RACISM AND RELIGIOUS BIGOTRY

Just as racism is a sad but ever-present facet of modern life in Britain, so too is religious bigotry. Whereas racial discrimination and abuse are crimes in this country, religious discrimination and abuse are not. Thus, many attacks against Muslim children are recorded as 'racist' when, in fact, they have been targeted because they are Muslims. **The present government is contemplating legislation to ban religious discrimination. The Queens's speech on 23rd November 2004 will include the proposed legislation** *(The Times, 18th November 2004).*

Schools should pay particular attention to protecting children from religious bigotry. Because of their often distinctive dress, Muslims are easy targets, particularly Muslim girls if they choose to wear ḥijāb (head covering).

If Muslims were to be recognised by the authorities as a distinct 'ethnic' group (albeit made up of people of many different racial origins), there would be some protection in law against abuse. Such recognition has been afforded to Jews and Sikhs, who may well be European or Asian respectively (though not necessarily so) but are defined in law as ethnic groups.

School staff (teachers and non-teachers alike) are requested to ensure that abuse of any kind directed against Muslim children is taken very seriously and dealt with accordingly. **This has become even more important after September 11, 2001 as Muslims are now targeted for abuse, subjected to stop and search, and suspected of terrorist involvment. Even prominent Muslims are deported on the baseless suspicion of terrorist links.**

## RAMAḌĀN

Ramaḍān is the ninth month of the Islāmic calendar – the month of fasting. It is a special time for all Muslims. Its completion is celebrated on the day of ʿĪdul Fiṭr.

Muslims fast from daybreak to sunset (about 2.50am to 9.25pm in June and 6.00am to 4.00pm in December in London). This means no eating or drinking during these hours.

Fasting is compulsory once a child has reached the age of puberty. Those who are ill or on a journey are excused, as are women during their monthly period; missed days are made up for later in the year.

### Starting out

Children practice fasting from a young age, depending on their development and the wishes of parents. They may begin by 'fasting' for a half day, until lunchtime, and then move on to the occasional full day. Some children may want to fast before their parents feel they are ready for it! Teachers, especially in primary schools, should try to find out *from parents* which children are fasting and when.

### PE

When it comes to exercise and physical exertion the basic rule is – don't overdo it! Young people inexperienced in fasting may not make sufficient allowance for this. During the month of Rama∂ān, children can take part in PE provided that they are not expected to over-exert themselves. Swimming should be avoided, because of the likelihood of accidentally swallowing water.

### Medication

Sometimes illness prevents fasting. A mild cold or headache probably won't be a problem, but if someone is too ill to fast then they should stop fasting until they recover sufficiently.

It is important that essential medication is taken when required. For example, asthmatics should use their inhaler if necessary. Young Muslims might try to 'tough it out', but they should not risk their health for fasting. Teachers who are concerned should consult parents, and may get further advice from local Muslim contacts or national Muslim organisations.

### Encouragement

Fasting in Rama∂ān is the fourth 'pillar' of Islām, an act of worship of great importance. During this month Muslims should be more spiritual, more caring and considerate, they should control their temper and refrain from using bad language. Encouragement from teachers can give a real boost to young people learning to fast. When necessary, teachers can also remind pupils that bad behaviour and fasting don't go together!

### Tarāwīḥ

Every night in Rama∂ān there are special, extra prayers called Tarāwīḥ. These are performed in congregation at the mosque or at home. Because of this extra commitment, it is helpful if teachers bear it in mind when deciding how much homework to set.

### Lailatul Qadr

There is a very special night in the last ten days of Rama∂ān called Lailatul Qadr (The Night of Power or Decrees). It is not known for sure exactly which day it is on, so Prophet Muḥammad ﷺ has recommended that

Muslims increase their efforts for all of the last ten days. This is the night when the Qur'ān was first revealed, and Allāh describes it as better than a thousand months. So for the last ten days many Muslims do extra prayers during the night.

### 'Īdul Fiṭr

The completion of the fasting month of Ramaḍān is celebrated on 'Īdul Fiṭr, the first day after Ramaḍān (see box below). The day starts with a light meal, then special congregational prayers that the whole family can go to. Muslims usually spend the rest of the day visiting relatives or friends, and eating special food. Children are given present or new clothes.

It is important to remember that Muslims come from many different cultures. Each has its own types of foods, its own style of dress, and its own way of celebrating.

## Guidance for Schools for the Month of Ramaḍān

1. Schools with substantial number of Muslim pupils and those with majority of Muslim pupils should have clearly laid down policy for the month of Ramaḍān which is based on lunar calender.

2. Schools should inform the kitchen staff that the number of children requiring lunch may be lower than normal. Any fasting Muslim child who is entitled to a free school meal should have the option of having packed lunch at the end of the school within the health and safety policy of the school.

3. Every effort should be made to provide fasting children access to rooms set aside for prayers or a quiet area away from the dining area to rest if they so wish during the lunch-break (preferably separate rooms for adolescent boys and girls).

4. Adequate arrangements should be in place to supervise the fasting children during Ramaḍān. These arrangments should be well publicised to parents, teachers and carers.

5. Where possible washing facilities should be available for pupils getting ready for their prayers (Ṣalāh).

6. Schools should be sympathetic to pupils' desire to offer prayers at prescribed times particularly to their need to Jumu'ah prayers.

7.  It will greatly help if major school events like parents evenings, open nights, Governor meetings, school tests and internal exams, school trips and inter-school sports events are avoided during Rama∂ān. On page 49 we have given the possible dates for the years 2004-2010.

## 8. P.E., Swimming and After school activities:

*   Muslim pupils who are fasting should not be asked to do anything which <u>they</u> or their parents / carers feel will break their fast. For primary school children, parents' / carers' approval should be sought before insisting on participation or exemption from an activity. For some pupils the interpretation of deliberately doing something that is prohibited also includes putting yourself in a situation where it is likely to happen e.g. if you go swimming it is likely that you will swallow some water.

*   When Rama∂ān is in winter organising activities after school may mean that Muslim children will be unable to take part because parents / carers will want them home in time to break their fast.

*   Children should not feel that they are being punished because of their need to go home immediately after school, e.g. they should not be excluded from school teams because they did not come to practice sessions during Rama∂ān.

*   An after school detention for a pupil who is fasting could mean that he/she is not able to break their fast on time. Pupils will accept the punishment for doing something wrong, but they may feel a sense of injustice if this leads to a situation where they are not able to carry out their religious duty. Relationships may be harmed. Lunch time detentions would solve this problem (Sec. 550B(4))b(iii) of Education Act 1997) .

*   Schools with a high percentage of Muslim pupils should suspend swimming lessons throughout Rama∂ān.

# Holidays for 'Īdul Fiṭr and 'Īdul A∂ḥā

*   As the day of 'Īd varies and some celebrations run over more than one day it is advisable to give pupils two days holiday for each Id unless it falls within an existing holiday period.

- Wherever possible schools should consult with the local Mosques, or the Council of mosques, to determine the exact days for holidays.

# Rama∂ān, 'Īdul Fiṭr, 'Īdul A∂ḥā Dates
# For The Years 2004 to 2010

These are the *approximate* dates of Islāmic events for the years 2004 to 2010:

| Year | Rama∂ān starts | 'Īdul Fiṭr | 'Īdul A∂ḥā |
|---|---|---|---|
| 2004-2005 | 15 Oct. 2004 | 13/14 Nov. 2004 | 21 Jan. 2005 |
| 2005-2006 | 5  Oct. 2005 | 3  Nov. 2005 | 10 Jan. 2006 |
| 2006 | 24 Sep. 2006 | 23 Oct. 2006 | 31 Dec. 2006 |
| 2007 | 13 Sep. 2007 | 13 Oct. 2007 | 20 Dec. 2007 |
| 2008 | 1 Sep. 2008 | 30 Sep. 2008 | 8 Dec. 2008 |
| 2009 | 21 Aug. 2009 | 20 Sep. 2009 | 27 Nov. 2009 |
| 2010 | 11 Aug. 2010 | 9 Sep. 2010 | 16 Nov.2010 |

The fasting month of *Rama∂ān* lasts until *'Īdul Fiṭr*. The celebrations for *'Īdul A∂ḥā* continue for up to four days. **Please note that Islāmic dates are subject to the sighting of the new moon, so the dates given are accurate only to within a day or two.**

## MADRASAHS/ SUPPLEMENTARY MUSLIM SCHOOLS

British Muslims recognise that an education system which is grappling to come to terms with the needs of a pluralistic society cannot be expected to provide a full Islāmic education for Muslim children in non-denominational maintained schools. Hence, over the past 50 years or so, madrasahs supplementary schools have been established.

Run in the evenings and at weekends, most madrasahs do not have adequate facilities. However, such self-help community projects should be encouraged by local authorities by giving financial assistance to overcome the problems they face, such as finding suitable premises, qualified teachers, teaching aids, etc. Any surplus school buildings or unused properties could be utilised by the community for madrasahs, nurseries, day centres and so on.

If local authorities could give this sort of help, whilst simultaneously providing for the religious, moral and spiritual needs of Muslim children in the maintained sector, there will be real improvement in their education.

## MUSLIM SCHOOLS

It is arguable whether Church of England plans to expand the number of church-run schools in the 21$^{st}$ century would ever have seen the light of day if not for the growth of the Muslim schools' sector in Britain. Despite the existence, since 1998, of a handful of full-time state-funded Muslim schools, they remain a controversial subject. So much so, that in the wake of the riots in the north of England in 2001, **the Home office report, chaired by Ted Cantle,** appeared to lay the blame for the lack of "integration" and thus the blame for the riots themselves on faith schools. The Cantle Report calmly overlooked the fact that the rioters in Bradford, for example, would have attended ordinary state schools, not Muslim boys' schools, because the latter do not exist in that city. The problems arose, therefore, out of an inadequate state system, not the presence of faith schools.

Such demonisation of Muslim schools challenges people to examine their own levels of acceptance and understanding of Islām and Muslims and, indeed, has led to a growing examination of the nature of British multi-cultural approaches to the education of our children.

Supporters of Cantle's conclusions suggest that Muslim schools are divisive at a time when "community cohesion" is the latest buzz phrase. Muslim children attending schools with an Islāmic ethos will not, the argument runs, be capable of living as British citizens in any meaningful way. The evidence suggests otherwise. Ex-pupils of Muslim schools, which have been around for almost 25 years now, are to be found in all walks of life, having gone through the system and emerged at the other end as young Muslim adults confident enough in their identity and self-esteem to play a full and active role at university and the work-place. They have not, and do not, live in a vacuum, especially in this internet age. The state-funding of Muslim schools in some areas, and the increasing acknowledgement by the authorities that those which wish to stay independent are fulfilling a crucial function, has created a more open and accepting arena within which

Muslim children are educated. Recognising that Muslim parents who opt for faith schools built around Islām also have valid aspirations for their children, is one way that local education authorities have sought to widen the options available in terms of parental choice, a concept that has been a cornerstone of education since 1/944.

Although some critics of Muslim schools accuse them of being 'Asian' enclaves, the schools themselves, of course, simply reflect the communities they serve, much as the local non-faith state schools do. **If a school is situated in a predominantly 'Asian' area, the pupils will be nearly all from an 'Asian' background. Schools in all-white areas also reflect the make-up of the local community. Muslim schools are no exception, although with the relatively recent migration of Muslim communities from around the Middle East, North and East Africa, Muslim schools are increasingly multi-racial in their intake. This is true, also, of the staff at these schools, but despite the multi-racial and often multicultural nature of Muslim schools, one thing binds staff and pupils together: the common belief in Islām, a faith for all people, regardless of race.**

In the eighties, the initial development of Muslim schools tended to be either at a primary level or for girls only at the secondary stage. The reasons for this largely revolved around two issues: cost and the perceived desire to protect girls who were regarded as being more vulnerable and open to abuse due to the distinctive nature of their dress requirements. The dispute over and banning of the ḥijāb in French schools indicates that nothing much has changed over the intervening years, at least across the channel and among opponents of Muslim schools who cite the "common sense approach" of the French authorities towards "blatant religious symbols" in supposedly "secular" schools. In a democracy this is itself a discriminatory argument: girls in Muslim schools do not suffer from the kind of discrimination and abuse that many face in non-faith schools; their academic progress benefits as a result. On a wider front, it is generally accepted that girls perform better and achieve higher grades in single-sex schools, at least up to the age of sixteen. Annual league tables regularly show single-sex schools at the top, for boys *and* girls.

The demand that schools should be strictly secular in nature, and claims that secularism is "neutral" form part of the effort to remove religion from public life and that, for believers of any faith, not least the Muslims, is simply unacceptable. A conscious decision not to practise, or to prevent others from practising, a religion is never a neutral position to take. Arguments against faith schools based on this premise, far from sounding rational and reasonable actually demonstrate a degree of compulsion of the kind proponents claim to find abhorrent in faith schools. The paradox is clear.

**Faith schools, and Muslim schools in particular, form a vibrant part of the overall education provision in Britain that allows for parental choice and a degree of religious pluralism that speaks well of traditional British values. A growing number of Muslim schools, state-funded and independent, are developing an enviable track record of academic success across the Key Stages, as well as an Islāmic ethos that nurtures young people in the faith of their community, preparing them for life in a wider society that is increasingly challenging to people of all faiths and none. That is the aim of all education and, as more and more Muslims begin to see the benefits of full-time Islāmic education for their children, places at Muslim schools are in great demand. Parents are aware that the dreams of returning one day to their places of origin, dreams held by themselves and their own parents and grandparents, no longer hold anything of value for their children, and that they must prepare them for life in this country. That alone is a wonderful incentive for Muslim schools to be at the cutting edge of educational development, to ensure that their pupils are more than capable of facing life in the global village that is today's world. It is a challenge that Muslim schools are embracing with enthusiasm, attracting many more supporters in the process** *(Source: What does Islām Say? Ibrahim Hewitt, 2004).*

## TRUANCY IN SCHOOLS

Truancy or unauthorised absence is a problem in British Schools. **Unauthorised absence in schools in the academic year 2003/2004 numbered 51,651 children per day** *(Source: National Statistics, DfES*

*SFR 33/2004, 16 September 2004*). This figure shows the scale of the problem.

Regular attendance and punctuality are important for getting a good education. The Department for Education and Skills (DfES) is putting a great emphasis to improve school attendance by combating truancy. A ten percent improvement target on 2002 figures has been set. **The Independent** reported on 11 February that this target is unlikely to be met and the DfES will abandon the target.

Muslim pupils in British Schools already suffer from a number of disadvantages, e.g. coming from low income families with poor housing, poor parental involvement in the child's education, insufficient incentive from school authorities and religious discrimination etc. **Pakistani and Bangladeshi communities perform less well than other pupils at all stages of compulsory education. Both communities are over-represented among pupils with the poorest qualifications.** *(Source: Monitoring Minority Protection in the EU: The situation of Muslims in the UK, Open Society Institute, 2002, page 100 (3.1.1. Education)).*

There has been some improvement in the performance of Muslim Pupils from these two communities during the last three to four years, but a lot yet remains to be achieved.

**One effective way of improving school attendance and combatting unauthorised absence is to develop a partnership between the local Mosques and the Schools in close liaison with the LEA. An innovative example is a project called 'Improving School Attendance in Partnership' (ISAP) based at the East London Mosque in the London borough of Tower Hamlets. Stephen Grix, corporate Director (Education) of the borough says in a publication of ISAP titled 'Putting faith into practice': "Attendance had gone up in the 12 schools and, where project workers worked with individual families, improvement rates have been between 5 and 7 percent"** *(P.7).*

## CONCLUSION

We hope that everyone involved in education will benefit from reading this publication. If the issues raised are dealt with sensitively, with goodwill and optimism, followed by positive action it will be a great contribution towards a better future for all of us.

For their part, Muslim parents should participate in all school activities which conform to the Islāmic principles of life. They should take an active, positive interest and make special efforts to visit schools to discuss their children's educational progress.

**British Muslim children themselves should set good standards of behaviour, discipline and academic excellence: "Actions speak louder than words" should be the motto.** Muslim children should lead by example (as, indeed, should their parents) and make plans for their careers so that they can achieve their full potential.

British Muslims are industrious and resourceful and our contribution to the richness of British society is borne by facts on the ground. Mosques, minarets and Muslim-owned businesses are now an integral part of multicultural Britain, despite the fact that Muslims face discrimination from all quarters. The number of madrasahs and full-time Muslim schools demonstrates the determination of the community to pass on its Islāmic faith and heritage.

There is no denying the fact that British Muslims are an established community to be treated as equal members of British society as a whole. It is unreasonable to expect us to assimilate and lose our identity; for a community with such a strong religious identity total assimilation is an absurdity. However, integration as full *and equal* members of a multicultural, multifaith Britain – without in any way jeopardising the community's religious identity – should be no problem.

**One way forward is for there to be a willingness on the part of those in authority to understand the educational needs of British Muslims and meet those needs with impartiality. Society can only flourish when discrimination ceases to exist and equality is established.**

APPENDIX *I*

# Circular 1/94: Religious Education & Collective Worship (DFEE, 31 January 1994)

## Aims of RE

16. Religious education in schools should seek: to develop pupils' knowledge, understanding and awareness of Christianity, as the predominant religion in Great Britian, and the other principal religions represented in the country; to encourage respect for those holding different beliefs; and to help promote pupils' spritual, moral, cultural and mental development.

## Right of Withdrawal

44. Nothing in the Education Act 1993 affects parents' rights, as established in the 1944 Act and re-enacted in the 1988 Act, to withdraw their children from RE if they wish. To summarise:

   *1*  **if the parent asks that a pupil should be wholly or partly** *excused from attending any RE at the school, then the school must comply;*

   *2*  *a pupil may, if the parent requests this, be withdrawn from the school premises to receive RE elsewhere, so long as the LEA, or in the case of a grant -maintained school, the governing body, is satisfied that this will not interfere with the child's attendance at school other than at the beginning or end of any school session;*

   *3*  *if a parent of a pupil attending an LEA -maintained county or equivalent grant-maintained school wishes him or her to receive RE according to the tenets of a particular religious denomination and this can not conveniently be provided elsewhere, the LEA or governing body, in the case of a grant-maintained school, is required to allow such education within the school provided it does* **not consider that because of special circumstances it would be unreasonable to do so, and does not have to meet the cost;**

   *4*  *where the parent of a child attending an LEA - maintained aided, special agreement, or equivalent grant - maintained school wishes that child to receive RE according to the agreed syllabus and the child cannot conveniently attend a school where the syllabus is in use, the governors (of if, in the case of LEA -maintained schools, they are unwilling to do so, the LEA) must make suitable arrangements unless they (or the LEA) considers that special circumstances would make it un reasonable to do so (See paragraph 44.2)*

45. **A school continues to be responsible for the supervision of any child withdrawn by its parent from RE, unless the child is lawfully receiving religious education elsewhere (paragraph 44.2)**

**Exercise of right of withdrawal**

46. **The parental right to withdraw a child from receiving RE should be freely exercisable and a school must give effect to any such request. Parents are not obliged to state their reasons for seeking withdrawal.**

47. The law doest not prescribe how religious education should be taught or organised in schools. LEAs and schools should bear in mind, however, that the way in which RE is organised must reflect the duty to teach the agreed syllabus or what is provided according to a trust deed, and that parents must be enabled to exercise their rights to request that their child should be excused from RE. This should not cause problems if RE is taught as a separate subject; but particular care will be needed to ensure that parents are able to exercise this right where schools, including primary schools, teach RE in an integrated form along with National Curriculum subjects (from which there is no right of withdrawal).

48. There will be occasions when spontaneous enquiries made by pupils on religious matters arise in other areas of the curriculum.. Circumstances will vary, but responses to such enquiries are unlikely to constitute RE within the meaning of the legislation and a parent would not be able to insist on a child being withdrawn every time issues relating to religion and spiritual values were raised.

49. Experience suggests that, to avoid misunderstanding, a head

teacher will find it helpful to establish with any parent wanting to exercise the right of withdrawal:

- The religious issues about which the parent would object to his or her child being taught
- *The practical implications of withdrawal*
- *The circumstances in which the school can reasonably be expected to accmmodate parental wishes (paragraph 48); and*
- *Whether the parent will require any advanced notice of such RE, and if so, how much.*

## 50. Aims of Collective Worship

Collective Worship in schools should aim to provide the opportunity for pupils to worship God, to consider spiritual and moral issues and to explore their own beliefs; to encourage participation and response, whether through active involvement in the presentation of worship or through listening to and joining in the worship offered; and to develop community spirit, promote a common ethos and shared values, and reinforce positive attitudes.

## Exemption from broadly Christian collective worship ('determinations')

68. The requirements described above (paragraphs 60-66), that collective worship should be wholly or mainly of a broadly Christian character, should be appropriate for most pupils across the country. The 'determination' procedure, however, allows these requirements to be lifted in respect of some or all of the pupils in a school where they are inappropriate. In determining this, the standing advisory council on RE (SACRE) is to have regard to any circumstances relating to the faith backgrounds of the pupils which are relevant for deciding what character of collective worship is appropriate.

69. The 1993 Act allows any grant-maintained school equivalent to a county school (i.e. to which section 7(1) of the 1988 Act applies) to apply for determination in similar circumstances to a county school.

## Applying for a determination

70. If the head teacher of a school considers that the requirements for

collective worship in paragraph 60. Before doing so the head teacher must consult the school's governing body who in turn may wish to seek the views of parents.

71. The head teacher's application may relate either to a clearly described and defined group or to the whole school. Before considering applying for a determination in relation to the whole school, however, care should be taken to safeguard the interests of any parents of children for whom broadly Christian collective worship would be appropriate. One factor which may inform a head teacher's decision to make an application to the SACRE is the extent of withdrawals from broadly Christian collective worship.

72. In considering whether to grant a head teacher's request, the SACRE must ensure that the proposed determination is justified by any relevant circumstances relating to the family backgrounds of the pupils concerned. When it has made a determination on the request - which can only take the form of acceptance or rejection without modification - it must communicate this in writing to the head teacher and state the date from which it should take effect.

73. Any determination made under these arrangements ends after 5 years, unless renewed by the SACRE. There must be a review by the SACRE no later than 5 years after any determination was introduced; and subsequently within 5 years of review. The head teacher may request an earlier review at any time, after consulting the governing body. The head teacher must be given an opportunity to make representations in any review and, in turn, is required to consult the governing body who may wish to seek the views of parents.

74. It is for each SACRE to decide how applications should be made, and to make available any necessary guidance to schools.

### Right of withdrawal

83. Nothing in the Education Act 1993 affects parents' rights, as established in the 1/944 Act and re-enacted in the 1988 Act, to withdraw their children from collective worship if they wish. To summarise:

   *1. it cannot be a condition of attendance at any maintained school that a pupil attends, or abstains from attending, any Sunday school or place of worship.*

2. *if the parent asks that a pupil should be wholly or partly excused from attending any religious worship at the school, then the school must comply. This includes alternative worship provided by a school as a result of a determination by a SACRE;*

3. *where the parent of any pupil who is a broader at a maintained school requests that the pupil be permitted to attend worship in accordance with the tenets of a particular religious denomination on Sundays or other holy days, or to receive religious education in accordance with such tenets outside school hours, the school's governing body shall make arrangements may be provided for on schools premises, but are not to entail expenditure by the LEA or, in the case a grant -maintained school, its governing body.*

A school continue to be responsible for the supervision of any child withdrawn by its parent from collective worship.

### Exercise of right of withdrawal

85. The parental right to withdraw a child from attending collective worship should be freely exercisable and a school must give effect to any such request. Parents are not obliged to state their reasons for seeking withdrawal.

86. The right of withdrawal from collective worship would normally be exercised through the physical withdrawal of the pupil from the place where the act of worship is taking place. Indeed the school could insist that this is the way the right is to be implemented. If, however, both the parent and the school agree that the pupil should be allowed to remain physically present during the collective worship but not take part in it, nothing in the law prevents this.

87. Experience suggests that, to avoid misunderstanding, a head teacher will find it helpful to establish with any parent wanting to exercise the right of withdrawal:
   - The elements of worship in which the parent would object to the child taking part;
   - The practical implications of withdrawal; and

- Whether the parent will require any advanced notice of such worship, and, if so, how much.

### Duty to establish SACRE and agreed syllabus conference

89. There are statutory duties on every LEA to establish:

1   *a permanent body, called a standing advisory council for religious education (SACRE), to advise the LEA on matters concerned with the provision of RE and collective worship; and*

2   *an occasional body which must be convened to produce and recommend an agreed syllabus for RE, called an agreed syllabus conference.*

## *Education Act 1996*

### 9. Pupils to be educated in accordance with parents' wishes.

In exercising or performing all their respective powers and duties under the Education Acts, the Secretary of State, local education authorities and the funding authorities shall have regard to the general principle **that pupils are to be educated in accordance with the wishes of their parents, so far as that is compatible with the provision of efficient instruction and training and the avoidance of unreasonable public expenditure.**

### Section 351.

### Collective worship

### (1) General duties in respect of the curriculum.

The curriculum for a school satisfies the requirements of this section if it is a balanced and broadly based curriculum which-

**(a) promotes the spiritual, moral, cultural, mental and physical development of pupils at the school and of society, and**

(b)  prepares pupils at the school for the opportunities, responsibilities and experiences of adult life.

### Section 352.

*(1) The curriculum for every maintained school shall comprise a basic curriculum which includes-*

*(c) in the case of a secondary school, provision for sex education for*

*all registered pupils at the school, and*

*(d) in the case of a special school, provision for sex education for all registered pupils at the school who are provided with secondary education.*

### Section 370.

### (1) Duty of local education authority to state policy.

A local education authority shall-

*(a) determine, and keep under review, their policy in relation to the secular curriculum for the county, voluntary and special schools maintained by them, and*

*(b) make, and keep up to date, a written statement of that policy.*

(2) In discharging their duty under subsection (1), the authority shall consider, in particular-

*(a) the range of the secular curriculum, and*

*(b) the balance between its different components.*

(3) In carrying out their functions under this Act or any other enactment, the authority shall have regard to their policy as expressed in their statement.

### Section 371.

### (1) Functions of governing body: county, controlled and maintained special schools.

This section applies to the articles of government for a county, controlled or maintained special school.

(3) The articles shall require the governing body-

*(a) to consider separately (while having regard to the local education authority's statement under section 370) the question whether sex education should form part of the secular curriculum for the school, and*

*(b) to make, and keep up to date, a separate written statement-*

    *(i)     of their policy with regard to the content and organisation ofthe relevant part of the curriculum, or*

    *(ii)     where they conclude that sex education should not form part*

*of the secular curriculum, of that conclusion.*

(8) In relation to sex education, this section has effect subject to section 404(3).

**Section 375.**

**Agreed syllabuses of religious education.**

(3) Every agreed syllabus shall reflect the fact that the religious traditions in Great Britain are in the main Christian whilst taking account of the teaching and practices of the other principal religions represented in Great Britain.

**Section 376.**

**(1) Religious education: county schools.**

In the case of a county school, the provision for religious education for pupils at the school which is required by section 352(1)(a) to be included in the school's basic curriculum is provision for **religious education in accordance with an agreed syllabus adopted for the school or for those pupils**.

**Section 378.**

**Religious education: aided and special agreement schools.**

(1) In the case of an aided or special agreement school, the provision for religious education for pupils at the school which is required by section 352(1)(a) to be included in the school's basic curriculum is provision for religious education-

    *(a) in accordance with any provisions of the trust deed relating to the school, or*

    *(b) where provision for that purpose is not made by such a deed, in accordance with the practice observed in the school before it became a voluntary school, or*

    *(c) in accordance with any arrangements made under subsection (2).*

(2) Where the parents of any pupils at an aided or special agreement school-

    *(a) desire them to receive religious education in accordance with any agreed syllabus adopted by the local education authority, and*

*(b) cannot with reasonable convenience cause those pupils to attend a school at which that syllabus is in use, arrangements shall be made (unless the authority are satisfied that because of any special circumstances it would be unreasonable to do so) for religious education in accordance with that syllabus to be given to those pupils in the school.*

(3) Religious education under any such arrangements shall be given during the times set apart for the giving of religious education in the school in accordance with the provision for that purpose included in the school's basic curriculum by virtue of section 352(1)(a).

(4) Any arrangements under subsection (2) shall be made by the governing body, unless the local education authority are satisfied that the governing body are unwilling to make them, in which case they shall be made by the authority.

(5) Subject to subsection (4), the religious education given to pupils at an aided or special agreement school shall be under the control of the governing body.

## Section 385.

### Collective worship.

(1) Subject to section 389, all pupils in attendance at a maintained school other than a maintained special school shall on each school day take part in an act of collective worship.

(2) The arrangements for the collective worship in a school required by this section may, in respect of each school day, provide for a single act of worship for all pupils or for separate acts of worship for pupils in different age groups or in different school groups.

(3) For the purposes of subsection (2) a "school group" is any group in which pupils are taught or take part in other school activities.

(4) Subject to subsection (6), the arrangements for the collective worship required by this section shall be made-

## Section 386.

(1) Subsections (2) to (6) apply-

> *(a) (subject to section 387) in relation to a county school, and*
>
> *(b) (subject to sections 383 and 387) in relation to a grant-maintained school in relation to which section 379 applies,*

**(2) The collective worship required in the school by section 385 shall be wholly or mainly of a broadly Christian character.**

## Section 389.

### Exceptions and special arrangements.

(1) If the parent of a pupil at a maintained school requests that he may be wholly or partly excused-

> *(a) from receiving religious education given in the school in accordance with the school's basic curriculum,*
>
> *(b) from attendance at religious worship in the school, or*
>
> *(c) both from receiving such education and from such attendance, the pupil shall be so excused until the request is withdrawn.*

(5) Where the parent of a pupil who is a boarder at a maintained school requests that the pupil be permitted-

> *(a) to receive religious education in accordance with the tenets of a particular religion or religious denomination outside school hours, or*
>
> *(b) to attend worship in accordance with such tenets on Sundays or other days exclusively set apart for religious observance by the religious body to which his parent belongs,*

the governing body shall make arrangements for giving the pupil reasonable opportunities for doing so.

**(6) Arrangements under subsection (5) may provide for making facilities for such education or worship available on the school premises, but the arrangements shall not entail expenditure by the responsible authority.**

## Section 403.

### Sex education: manner of provision.

*(1) The local education authority, governing body and head teacher shall take such steps as are reasonably practicable to secure that*

*where sex education is given to any registered pupils at a maintained school, it is given in such a manner as to encourage those pupils to have due regard to moral   considerations and the value of family life.*

*(2) In subsection (1) "maintained school" includes a maintained special school established in a hospital.*

## Section 404.

## Sex education: statements of policy.

*(1) The governing body of a maintained school shall-*
  *(a) make, and keep up to date, a separate written statement of their policy with regard to the provision of sex education, and*
  *(b) make copies of the statement available for inspection (at all reasonable times) by parents of registered pupils at the school and provide a copy of the statement free of charge to any such parent who asks for one.*

## Section 405.

## Exemption from sex education.

If the parent of any pupil in attendance at a maintained school   requests that he may be wholly or partly excused from receiving sex education at the school, the pupil shall, except so far as such education is comprised in the National Curriculum, be so excused accordingly until the request is withdrawn.

## Section 411.

## Parental preferences.

(1)  A local education authority shall make arrangements for enabling the parent of a child in the area of the authority-
  *(a) to express a preference as to the school at which he wishes education to be provided for his child in the exercise of the authority's functions, and*
  *(b) to give reasons for his preference.*

(2) Subject to subsection (3) and section 430(2) (co-ordinated admis-

sion arrangements), a local education authority and the governing body of a county or voluntary school shall comply with any preference expressed in accordance with arrangements made under subsection (1).

(3) The duty imposed by subsection (2) does not apply-

  (a) *if compliance with the preference would prejudice the provision of efficient education or the efficient use of resources;*

  (b) *if the preferred school is an aided or a special agreement school and compliance with the preference would be incompatible with any arrangements between the governing body and the local education authority made under section 413; or*

  (c) *if the arrangements for admission to the preferred school are based wholly or partly on selection by reference to ability or aptitude and compliance with the preference would be incompatible with selection under the arrangements.*

(4) Where the arrangements for the admission of pupils to a school maintained by a local education authority provide for applications for admission to be made to (or to a person acting on behalf of) the governing body of the school, a parent who makes such an application shall be regarded for the purposes of subsection (2) as having expressed a preference for that school in accordance with arrangements made under subsection (1).

(5) The duty imposed by subsection (2) in relation to a preference expressed in accordance with arrangements made under subsection (1) shall apply also in relation to-

  (a) any application for the admission to a school maintained by a local education authority of a child who is not in the area of the authority, and

  (b) any application made by a parent as mentioned in section 438(4) or 440(2) (application for a particular school to be specified in a school attendance order);

  and references in subsection (3) to a preference and a preferred school shall be construed accordingly.

(6) No prejudice shall be taken to arise for the purposes of subsection

(3) (a) from the admission to a county or voluntary school in a school year of a number of pupils in a relevant age group which does not exceed-

(a) the relevant standard number, or

(b) the admission number fixed in accordance with section 416, whichever is the greater.

(7) In this Chapter "the relevant standard number", in relation to a county or voluntary school, a relevant age group and a school year, means the standard number applying under sections 417 to 420 to the school in relation to that age group and year.

(8) In this section "child" includes a person who has not attained the age of 19.

**Section 444.**

**Offence: failure to secure regular attendance at school of registered pupil.**

**(1)** If a child of compulsory school age who is a registered pupil at a school fails to attend regularly at the school, his parent is guilty of an offence.

(2) Subsections (3) to (6) below apply in proceedings for an offence under this section in respect of a child who is not a boarder at the school at which he is a registered pupil.

(3) The child shall not be taken to have failed to attend regularly at the school by reason of his absence from the school-

(a) *with leave,*

(b) *at any time when he was prevented from attending by reason of sickness or any unavoidable cause, or*

(c) **on any day exclusively set apart for religious observance by the religious body to which his parent belongs.**

# Education Act 1997

**Section 550B**

**Detention outside school hours lawful despite absence of parental consent.**

(1) Where a pupil to whom this section applies is required on discipli-

nary grounds to spend a period of time in detention at his school after the end of any school session, his detention shall not be rendered unlawful by virtue of the absence of his parent's consent to it if the conditions set out in subsection (3) are satisfied.

(2) This section applies to any pupil who has not attained the age of 18 and is attending-

(a) *a school maintained by a local education authority;*

(b) *a grant-maintained or grant-maintained special school; or*

(c) *a city technology college or city college for the technology of the arts.*

(3) The conditions referred to in subsection (1) are as follows-

(a) *the head teacher of the school must have previously determined, and have-*

(i) *made generally known within the school, and*

(ii) *taken steps to bring to the attention of the parent of every person who is for the time being a registered pupil there,*

*that the detention of pupils after the end of a school session is one of the measures that may be taken with a view to regulating the conduct of pupils;*

(b) *the detention must be imposed by the head teacher or by another teacher at the school specifically or generally authorised by him for the purpose;*

(c) *the detention must be reasonable in all the circumstances; and*

(d) *the pupil's parent must have been given at least 24 hours' notice in writing that the detention was due to take place.*

(4) In determining for the purposes of subsection (3)(c) whether a pupil's detention is reasonable, the following matters in particular shall be taken into account-

(a) *whether the detention constitutes a proportionate punishment in the circumstances of the case; and*

(b) *any special circumstances relevant to its imposition on the pupil which are known to the person imposing it (or of which he ought reasonably to be aware) including in particular-*

(i)     *the pupil's age,*

(ii)    **any special educational needs he may have,**

(iii)   **any religious requirements affecting him,** *and*

(iv)    *where arrangements have to be made for him to travel from the school to his home, whether suitable alternative arrangements can reasonably be made by his parent.*

(5) Section 572, which provides for the methods by which notices may be served under this Act, does not preclude a notice from being given to a pupil's parent under this section by any other effective method."

# School Standard and Framework Act 1998

## Duty to secure due provision of religious education.

### Section 69

(1) Subject to section 71, in relation to any community, foundation or voluntary school-

   *(a) the local education authority and the governing body shall exercise their functions with a view to securing, and*

   *(b) the head teacher shall secure, that religious education is given in accordance with the provision for such education included in the school's basic curriculum by virtue of section 352(1)(a) of the Education Act 1996.*

(2) Schedule 19 has effect for determining the provision for religious education which is required by section 352(1)(a) of that Act to be included in the basic curriculum of schools within each of the following categories, namely-

   *(a) community schools and foundation and voluntary schools which do not have a religious character,*

   *(b) foundation and voluntary controlled schools which have a religious character, and*

   *(c) voluntary aided schools which have a religious character.*

(3) For the purposes of this Part a foundation or voluntary school has a religious character if it is designated as a school having such a character by an order made by the Secretary of State.

(4) An order under subsection (3) shall state, in relation to each school designated by the order, the religion or religious denomination in accordance with whose tenets religious education is, or may be, required to be provided at the school in accordance with Schedule 19 (or, as the case may be, each such religion or religious denomination).

(5) The procedure to be followed in connection with-

    *(a) the designation of a school in an order under subsection (3), and*

    *(b) the inclusion in such an order, in relation to a school, of the statement required by subsection (4), shall be specified in regulations.*

**Religious worship**

**Section 70**

**Requirements relating to collective worship.**

(1) Subject to section 71, each pupil in attendance at a community, foundation or voluntary school shall on each school day take part in an act of collective worship.

(2) Subject to section 71, in relation to any community, foundation or voluntary school-

    *(a) the local education authority and the governing body shall exercise their functions with a view to securing, and*

    *(b) the head teacher shall secure, that subsection (1) is complied with.*

(3) Schedule 20 makes further provision with respect to the collective worship required by this section, including provision relating to-

    *(a) the arrangements which are to be made in connection with such worship, and*

    *(b) the nature of such worship.*

# *The Ethical Standards in Public Life Bill, Scotland, 2000*

*The Scottish Parliament voted to repeal Section 28 of the Local Government Act by 99 votes to 17 on 21st June 2000. The legislation*

*was part of the Ethical Standards in Public Life Bill. Section 28, stated that a local authority is not permitted to "…promote the teaching in any maintained school of the acceptability of homosexuality as a pretended family relationship." The Act did not apply directly to schools but governed Local Authorities.*

## Learning and Skills Bill 2000

**Clause 117** *of the bill updates and amends the Education Act 1996*

*Local education authorities no longer have any responsibility for sex education in maintained schools; this now rests with the school's governing body and head teacher. [(2) and (3)]*

## National Science Curriculum.

### Sex and Relationship Education (SRE) (Ref: DfES 0706/2001)

### Key Stage 1

- *Animals, including humans, move, feed, grow, use their sense and reproduce*

- *Children should recognise and name the main external parts of the human body.*

- *That human can produce offspring and these grow into adults*

- *Children should recognise similarities and differences between themselves and other and treat others with sesitivly*

### Key Stage 2

- *Life process common to humans include nutrition, growth and reproduction*

- *The main stages of human lifecystyle.*

### Key Stage 3

- *Fertilization in humans is the fusion of a male and female cell*

- *Student should know the physical and emotional changes that take place during adolescence*

- *The human reproductive cycle, including the menstrual cycle and fertilisation*

- *How the growth and reproduction of bacteria and the replication of viruses can effects human health.*

### Key Stage 4

- *Hormonal control in humans, including the effects of sex hormones*

- *Medical uses of hormones, including the control and promotion of fertility*

- *How sex is determined in humans.*

*[Sex and relationship education (SRE) (Ref: DfES 0706/2001]*

# Sexual Offences (Amendment) Bill, 2001

*The Sexual Offences (Amendment) Bill came into effect on January 8th 2001, and reduced the age of sexual consent for gay men from 18 to 16 in England, Wales and Scotland. In Northern Ireland, the age of consent for gay men was brought into line with the heterosexual age of consent at 17.*

# Education Act, 2002

### 19  Governing bodies

(1) Each maintained school shall have a governing body, which shall be a body corporate constituted in accordance with regulations.

(2) Regulations shall provide for a governing body to consist of-

    *(a) persons elected or appointed as parent governors,*

    *(b) persons elected or appointed as staff governors,*

    *(c) persons appointed as local education authority governors,*

    *(d) except in the case of a voluntary aided school, persons appointed as community governors,*

    *(e) in the case of a foundation school, a foundation special school or a voluntary school, persons appointed as foundation governors or*

*partnership governors, and*

*(f) such other persons as may be prescribed.*

## 84  Curriculum requirements for first, second and third key stages

(1) For the first, second and third key stages, the National Curriculum for England shall comprise the core and other foundation subjects specified in subsections (2) and (3), and shall specify attainment targets, programmes of study and assessment arrangements in relation to each of those subjects for each of those stages.

(2) The following are the core subjects for the first, second and third key stages-

*(a) mathematics,*

*(b) English, and*

*(c) science.*

(3) The following are the other foundation subjects for the first, second and third key stages-

*(a) design and technology,*

*(b) information and communication technology,*

*(c) physical education,*

*(d) history,*

*(e) geography,*

*(f) art and design,*

*(g) music, and*

*(h) in relation to the third key stage-*

> *(i) citizenship, and*

> *(ii) a modern foreign language.*

(4) In this section "modern foreign language" means a modern foreign language specified in an order made by the Secretary of State or, if the order so provides, any modern foreign language.

(5) An order under subsection (4) may-

*(a) specify circumstances in which a language is not to be treated as a foundation subject, and*

*(b) provide for the determination under the order of any question arising as to whether a particular language is a modern foreign language.*

(6) The Secretary of State may by order amend subsections (2) to (5).

## *Local Government Act 1988*

### Section 28

*(1) The following section shall be inserted after section 2 of the Local Government Act 1986 (prohibition of political publicity)—*

*"Prohibition on*    *2A.—(1) A local authority shall not—*
*promoting*            *(a) intentionally promote homosexuality or publish*
*homosexuality*               *material with the intention of promoting*
*by teaching or*              *homosexuality;*
*by publishing*           *(b) promote the teaching in any maintained school of*
*material*                    *the acceptability of homosexuality as a pretended*
                                   *family relationship.*

*(2) Nothing in subsection (1) above shall be taken to prohibit the doing of anything for the purpose of treating or preventing the spread of disease.*

## *Local Government Act 1988, England and Wales (Amendment) Bill 2003*

*The repeal of Section 28 of the local Government act was voted for by the House of commons in March 2003 and by the House of Lords in July 2003. It received its Royal Assent on September 18th 2003.*

## Appendix II

From: The Minister of State,
   Department of Education & Science,
   Elizabeth House, York Road, London, SE1 7PH.

To:  Ghulam Sarwar, Esq.,
   Director, The Muslim Educational Trust,
   130, Stroud Green Road, London, N4 3RZ.

24 NOV 1989

Dear Mr. Sarwar,

Thank you for your letter of 3 November to John MacGregor concerning Collective Worship in schools. I am replying as this falls within my area of ministerial responsibility.

It would appear from your letter that the concern felt by some Muslim parents over who is responsible for providing worship for pupils covered by a SACRE determination arises from a misunderstanding of the provisions in the Education Reform Act and the guidance offered in Circular 3/89.

Section 12 of the ERA allows head teachers of county schools, after consultation with the governing body, to apply to the SACRE for a determination which lifts the requirement for the school to provide worship which is wholly or mainly of a broadly Christian character, where the head teacher feels that requirement is inappropriate. An application may be made in respect of the whole school, or a group of pupils at the school. If a determination is granted, worship must still be provided for those pupils covered by the determination, unless their parents request that they be withdrawn. This worship may be distinctive of any particular faith, but may not be distinctive of a particular religious denomination. The precise content of the worship provided to pupils covered by a determination is the responsibility of the head teacher. The SACRE has no power to lay down what should be the nature of worship provided as a result of a determination.

The responsibility for organising all statutory Collective Worship – which includes any alternative worship provided as a result of a determination by a SACRE – and for meeting any necessary costs, lies with the LEA or the school, depending on whether or not the school has a delegated budget.

Paragraph 42 of Circular 3/89 does not, however, relate to statutory Collective Worship. That paragraph is concerned only with cases where parents request schools to allow <u>non</u>-statutory RE or Collective Worship to be provided for pupils who have been withdrawn from any statutory RE or worship. It is entirely for the school to decide whether or not to allow non-statutory RE or worship. Where a school agrees to such a request, any arrangements made must not entail any additional cost to the school.

I hope this clears up any misunderstanding.

Yours sincerely,

Angela Rumbold (signed)

# APPENDIX III

Selected booklist suitable for teacher/pupil use. Most books listed are available direct from the publishers or from Muslim bookshops.

## List 1
## Books suitable for teacher use

*The Holy Qur'ān,* English translation and commentary by Abdullah Yusuf Ali, revised and edited by the Presidency of Islāmic Research, Ifta, Call and Guidance, King Fahad Holy Qur'ān Printing Complex, Saudi Arabia.

*Towards Understanding the Qur'ān,* volumes 1 - 7, S. A. A. Mawdudi, translated by Zafar Ishaq Ansari, The Islāmic Foundation, Markfield Confrence Centre, Ratby Lane, MARKFIELD, Leicestershire LE67 9SY.

*The Qur'ān: Basic Teachings,* Ahmad, Irving and Ahsan, The Islāmic Foundation. ISBN 0 860370 222-7

*In the Shade of the Qur'ān*, vol. I - VII Sayyid Qutb, The Islāmic Foundation.

*Muḥammad*, Martin Lings, Allen & Unwin. ISBN 0 04 297042-3

*The Eternal Message of Muḥammad*, Abdur Rahman Azzam, Quartet. ISBN 0 704332 03 5

*The Meccan Crucible*, Zakaria Bashir, The Islāmic Foundation. ISBN 086037 2049

*Hijra: Story and Significance,* Zakaria Bashir, The Islāmic Foundation. ISBN 0 860371 24 7

*Muḥammad - Man and Prophet-* Adil Salahi, Islāmic Foundation. ISBN 0 86037-322-3

*Islām: Its meaning and message,* K. Ahmed (ed.), The Islāmic Foundation. ISBN 0 860370 00 3

*What everyone should know about Islām and Muslims,* Suzanne Haneef, Kazi Publications, Chicago.

*Islām in Focus,* Hammudah Abdal 'Ati, American Trust Publications, ISBN 0 892590 00 9

*Towards Understanding Islām,* S. A. A. Mawdudi, The Islāmic Foundation. ISBN 0 86037 065-8

*The Cultural Atlas of Islām,* Ismail Faruqi and Lois Lamya Faruqi,

Macmillan.

*Principles of State and Government in Islām*, Muḥammad Asad, Dar al-Andalus, Gibralter.

**Social Justice in Islām,** Sayyid Qutb, Octagon Books, New York.

*Islāmic Teachings Course*, Sarah Sheriff, Islāmia Schools Trust, ISBN 0947879 02-1/01-3

*Approaches to Islām,* Richard Tames & John Murray. ISBN 0719539 14 5

*Al-Dhabh (Slaying animals the Islāmic way),* G. M. Khan, Ta Ha Publishers, ISBN 0 907461 14X

*Islāmic Health Rules,* Dr. S. M. Darsh, Ta Ha Publishers.

*Islām in Britain,* Dr. Zaki Badawi, Ta Ha Publishers.

**Sex Education: The Muslim Perspective,** Ghulam Sarwar, The Muslim Educational Trust, ISBN 0 907261 41 8.

**What does Islām say?** Ibrahim Hewitt, The Muslim Educational Trust, ISBN 0 907261 42 6

*The Islāmic Ruling on Music and Singing*, Abu Bilal Mustafa Al-Kanadi, P. O. Box 6156, Jeddah, 21442, Saudi Arabia.

*Inner Dimensions of Islāmic Worship*, Imam Al-Ghazali, translated by Muhtar Holland, The Islāmic Foundation.

*The Duties of Brotherhood in Islām*, Imam Al-Ghazali, translated by Muhtar Holland, The Islāmic Foundation.

*Human Rights in Islām,* Abul A'la Mawdudi, The Islāmic Foundation.

*Woman in Islām,* B. Aisha Lemu & Fatima Heeren, The Islāmic Foundation.

*The Muslim Minorities,* M. Ali Kettani, The Islāmic Foundation.

*Young Muslims in a Multi-Cultural Society,* Muḥammad Anwar, The Islāmic Foundation.

**The Case for Muslim Voluntary Aided Schools,** J. M. Halstead, The Islāmic Academy, ISBN 0 948295 07 4

*Muslims in the West: The Message and Mission*, Syed Abul Hasan Ali Nadwi, The Islāmic Foundation. ISBN 086037 1301

*Fiqh us-Sunnah,* volumes 1 - 4, As-Sayyid Sabiq, American Trust Publications, USA.

*What every Christian Should Know About Islām,* Ruqaiyyah Waris Maqsood, Islāmic Foundation. ISBN 0 86037 375-4

## List 2
## Books suitable for pupil use

a.   Secondary level

*The Qur'ān (Part 30) in plain English for children and young people,* The Islāmic Foundation. ISBN 0 86037 233 2

*The Qur'ān – translation and study,* parts 1 - 5, Jamal un Nisa bint Rafai, Ta Ha Publishers.

*Forty Hadith Qudsi,* selected & translated by E. Ibrahim & D. Johnson Davies), Holy Qur'ān Publishing House, P. O. Box 2409, Damascus, Syria.

*Forty Hadith,* Imam Nawawi (trans. E. Ibrahim & D. Johnson Davies), Holy Qur'ān Publishing House.

*The Life of the Prophet Muḥammad,* Azzam & Gouverneur, Islāmic Texts Society, ISBN 0 946621 02 0

*Islām: Beliefs and Teachings,* Ghulam Sarwar, The Muslim Educational Trust, ISBN 0 907261 38 8

*Companions of the Prophet, Books 1, 2 & 3,* AbdulWahid Hamid, ISBN 0 948196 00 9/017/025

*Muḥammad – Aspects of his Biography,* Z. Sardar, The Islāmic Foundation, ISBN 0 860370 23 2

*A Day with the Prophet,* Ahmad von Denffer, The Islāmic Foundation, ISBN 0 860371 21 2

*The Beginner's Book of Salah,* Ghulam Sarwar, The Muslim Educational Trust, ISBN 0 907261 39 6

*Examining Religions: Islām,* Rosalyn Kendrick, Heinemann Educational, ISBN 0 435303 14 7

*Islām the Natural Way,* A. W. Hamid, MELS, ISBN 0 948196 09 2

*The Lawful and the Prohibited in Islām,* Yusuf Al-Qaradawi, American Trust Publications, ISBN 0 89259 016 5

*Morals and Manners in Islām,* Marwan Ibrahim Al-Kaysi, The Islāmic Foundation, ISBN 0 860371 68 9

*What does Islām say?* Ibrahim Hewitt, MET, ISBN 0 907261 42-6

*The Muslim Woman's Handbook,* Huda Khattab, Ta Ha Publishers.

*Marvellous Stories from the Life of Muḥammad,* Mardijah A. Tarantino,

The Islāmic Foundation, ISBN 0 86037 103 4

*Selection from Hadith,* A. Hamid Siddiqy, Islāmic Book Publishers, Kuwait.

*Capitalism, Socialism and Islām,* Abul A'lā Mawdudi, Islāmic Book Publishers, Kuwait.

*Modesty and Chastity in Islām,* Muḥammad Zafeeruddin Nadvi, Islāmic Book Publishers, Kuwait.

*Muslims in Europe,* Dr. S. M. Darsh, Ta Ha Publishers.

*The Miracle of Life,* Fatima. M. D'oyen, The Islaim Foundation, ISBN 0 86037-355 X

### b. Primary level

***Islām for Younger People,*** Ghulam Sarwar, The Muslim Educational Trust, ISBN 0 907261 40 X

*Islāmic Quiz Books 1 & 2,* Jamal un-Nisa, Ta Ha Publishers

*Colouring Book 1 (Mosques of the world),* Ta Ha Publishers

*Marvellous Stories from the Life of Muḥammad,* Mardijah A. Tarantino, The Islāmic Foundation.

*The Longing Heart: Story of Abu Dhar,* Khurram Murad, The Islāmic Foundation.

*The Long Search: Story of Salman the Persian,* Khurram Murad, The Islāmic Foundation.

*The Courageous Children,* Ayesha Abdullah Scott, The Islāmic Foundation.

*Muslim Poems for Children,* Mymona Hendricks, The Islāmic Foundation.

Books from the ***Muslim Children's Library*** series, The Islāmic Foundation

All titles in **bold** print should be an essential part of any school library.

## Audio-Visual Material

A vaiety of Audio-Casettes, Video, CD's, Computer Games are available from:

1)  **Islāmic Foundation**
    Publications Unit
    Markfield Conference Centre
    Ratby Lane
    MARKFIELD
    Leicestershire LE67 9SY
    01530 249230

2)  **Ta Ha Publishers**
    1 Wynne Road
    LONDON SW9 0BB
    020 7737 7266

3)  **Sound Vision**
    86 Kingsley Road
    HOUNSLOW
    Middlesex TW3 1QA
    020 8570 1999

4)  **Iqra Book Center**
    7450 Skokie Blvd.
    Skokie
    IL 60077
    00 1 847 673 0004

There are many bookshops which sell Audio-Visual materials on Islām.

## Appendix IV

Muslim Bookshops in Britain stocking a wide range of books (including those listed in

*Appendix III*) in addition to artefacts, posters, tapes, etc.

**Al-Furqaan Bookshop**
102 Whitechapel Road LONDON E1 1JE
020 7247 7439

**Al-Kitab Bookshop**
(Jamiah Mosque –
UK Islāmic Mission)
Brownlow Road West Ealing
LONDON W13 0SQ
020 8840 4140

**Al-Madina Bookshop**
392 Green Street
Upton Park LONDON E13 9AP
020 8586 9400

**Al-Madina Publications**
13 Carlton Avenue
BATLEY West Yorkshire WF17 7AQ
01924 444666

**Al-Muntada Al-Islāmi Bookshop**
7 Bridges Place
Parsons Green LONDON SW6 4HW
020 7736 9060

**Amsons Bookshop**
209 Dunstable Road
LUTON Bedfordshire LU1 1DD
01582 734 627

**Amsons Bookshop**
353 - 355 Coventry Road
Small Heath BIRMINGHAM B10 0SN
0121 773 6446

**Asian Book & Music Centre**
177 Alison Street GLASGOW G42 8RX
0141 423 9440
**Bigland Islāmic Book Service**
C/O Darul Ummah 56 Bigland Street
LONDON E1 2ND
020 7790 9779

**Book Centre**
**Express House**
White Abbey Road, BRADFORD
West Yorkshire BD8 8EJ
01274 727864

**Brick Lane Music House**
74 Brick Lane LONDON E1 6RL
 020 7247 2547

**Choudhry Fashion**
266 High Street North
Manor Park LONDON E12 6SB
020 8552 9677

**Dar Al Taqwa**
7a Melcombe Street
LONDON NW1 6AE
020 7935 6385

**Darul Kutub Islāmic Book Centre**
139 Albert Drive
Pollockshields GLASGOW G41 2NE
0141 423 6665

**Darul-Kutub**
70 South Street, Savile Town
DEWSBURY,
West Yorkshire WF12 9NG
01924 488082

**East London Mosque**
Book Centre 96 Whitechapel Road
LONDON E1 1JQ
020 7247 4665

**Indian Record House**
41 The Broadway
SOUTHALL MiddlesexUB1 1JY
020 8574 4739

**Iqra Books**
65 South Road
SOUTHALL Middlesex UB1 1SQ
020 8867 989

**Iqra Books and Stationery**
301 Normanton Road
Normanton DERBY DE23 6UU
01332 201 814

**Islāmic Book Centre**
71 Holmrook Road
PRESTON Lancashire PR1 6SS
01772 461074

**Islāmic Book Centre**
19 Carrington Street
GLASGOW Strathclyde G4 9AJ
0141 332 2811/0141 331 1119

**Islāmic Book Centre**
8 Forest Street, NELSON
Lancashire BB9 7NB
01282 694471

**Islāmic Foundation**
Publications Unit
Markfield Conference Centre
Ratby Lane MARKFIELD
Leicestershire LE67 9SY
01530 249230

**Islāmic Vision**
434 Coventry Road
Small Heath BIRMINGHAM
West Midlands B10 0UG
0121 773 0137

**Kashmir Book Centre**
523 Stratford Road
Sparkhill BIRMINGHAM
West Midlands B11 4LP
0121 773 6634

**London Iman Centre**
16 Sewell Road, Abbey Wood
LONDON SE2   9XN
020 8311 6752

**Madina Book Centre**
343 Normanton Road
Normanton DERBY Derbyshire
01332 368002

**Muslim Printers & Booksellers**
423 Stratford Road, Sparkhill
BIRMINGHAM  West Midlands B11 4LB
0121 773 8301

**Muslim Bookshop**
233 Seven Sisters Road
LONDON N4 2DA
020 7272 5170

**Mizan Books**
119 Burford Road, Forest Fields
NOTTINGHAM Nottinghamshire
NG7 6BA
0115 942 2228

**Multi Cultural Book Services**
Bradford Unit 33
Carlisle Business Centre
60 Carlisle Road BRADFORD
BD8 8BD
01274 544 158

**Olive Tree International**
61 Renshaw Street LIVERPOOL LI 2SJ

**Rolex Trading Company**
Rashid House, Westgate
BRADFORD. West Yorkshire
BD1 3AA
01274 731908

**Rolex Books (Manchester)**
81-83 Wilmslow Road
Rusholme MANCHESTER
M14 5SU
0161 225 4448

**Rochdale Dawah Centre**
19 Sitton Street
ROCHDALE OL16 2DZ

**Safa Books**
117 Whitechapel Road
LONDON E1 1DT
020 8208 4815

**Sakina Bookshop**
204 Uxbridge Road, Shepherds Bush
LONDON W12 7JD
020 8743 1326

**Usmani Islamic Books**
129 The Broadway, Perry Barr
BIRMINGHAM B20 3ED

**Zainab Foundation Bookshop**
Al-Baraka House 18-20 Park Street
SLOUGH Berkshire SL1 1PD
01753 533511

**Zam Zam Bookshop**
Unit 5 388 Green Street
LONDON E13 9AB
020 8470 1300

## OVERSEAS BOOKSHOPS

**Iqra Book Center**
7450 Skokie Blvd.
Skokie
IL 60077, USA
00 1 847 673 0004

**Islamic Bookstore** - Australia
165 Haldon St
Lakemba NSW 2195
AUSTRALIA
00612 975 84040

**Ḥalālco Books**
155 Hillwood Avenue
Falls Church
Virginia
VA 22046, USA
00 1 703 532 3202

**Islamic Books & Clothing**
162 Sydney Road
Coburg Victoria 3058
AUSTRALIA
00 61 3 947 888 53

**ICNA Book Service**
166-26, 89th Avenue
Jamaica
New York
NY 11432, USA
00 1 718 657 4090

**Original Path Books**
2-3415 Dixie Road,
Unit 505 Mississauga
Ontario L4Y 4J6
CANADA
001 905 625 6619

## MET PUBLICATIONS

1. ***Islām Beliefs & Teachings***                             £6.50
   by Ghulam Sarwar, 7th edition, 2003, pp240

2. ***Islām for Younger People***                              £3.00
   by Ghulam Sarwar, 4th edition (New design), 2003, pp64

3. ***The Beginner's Book of Ṣalāh***                          £3.00
   by Ghulam Sarwar, 6th edition, 2003, pp64

4. ***Sex Education – The Muslim Perspective***                £3.75
   by Ghulam Sarwar, 4th edition, 2004, pp72

5. ***What does Islām say?***                                  £3.75
   by Ibrahim B. Hewitt, 4th edition, 2004, pp64

6. ***Islāmic Education: its meanings, problems & prospects*** £2.50
   by Ghulam Sarwar 1st edition, 2001, pp56

7. ***British Muslims & Schools***                             £3.75
   by Ghulam Sarwar, 3rd edition, 2004, pp84

Plus a selection of full-colour posters. A catalogue is available on request.
Prices include postage in the UK

*Please send your orders, with payment, to:*

## The Muslim Educational Trust
**130 Stroud Green Road, London N4 3RZ**
**Tel: 020 7272 8502  Fax: 020 7281 3457**
*www.muslim-ed-trust.org.uk     email:info@muslim-ed-trust.org.uk*